Crossing Border Street

Crossing Border Street

A Civil Rights Memoir

Peter Jan Honigsberg

UNIVERSITY OF CALIFORNIA PRESS

Berkeley   Los Angeles   London

University of California Press
Berkeley and Los Angeles, California

University of California Press, Ltd.
London, England

Photograph on previous page: Robert Hicks (second from
left) and other demonstrators chant "Black Power" during a
two-day march from Bogalusa in 1966. Courtesy AP/Wide
World Photos.

Library of Congress Cataloging-in-Publication Data

Honigsberg, Peter Jan.
    Crossing Border Street : a civil rights memoir / Peter
    Jan Honigsberg.
        p.   cm.
    Includes index.
    ISBN 0-520-22147-8 (cloth : alk. paper)
        1. Afro-Americans—Civil rights—Louisiana—
    History—20th century.   2. Afro-Americans—Legal
    status, laws, etc.—Louisiana—History—20th century.
    3. Afro-American civil rights workers—Louisiana—
    History—20th century.   4. Louisiana—Race relations.
    5. Honigsberg, Peter Jan.   6. Civil rights workers—
    Louisiana—Biography.   7. Law students—Louisiana—
    Biography.   I. Title.

    F376.H66 2000
    976.3'00496073'0092—dc21
    [B]   99-087300

Manufactured in the United States of America

09 08 07 06 05 04 03 02 01 00
10 9 8 7 6 5 4 3 2 1

The paper used in this publication meets the minimum re-
quirements of ANSI/NISO Z39.48-1992 (R 1997) (*Permanence
of Paper*).

*For Robert Hicks and Gayle Jenkins
and in memory of A.Z. Young*

The actual name of the street referred to in the title of this memoir is North Border Drive. But I have always thought of it as "Border Street," a far more evocative and poignant image of the real and metaphorical boundaries that kept the black and white communities apart.

CONTENTS

ILLUSTRATIONS

A MEMORY

I have written a memoir, not a history. In writing it, I have tried to remain true to the records and chronology of the civil rights movement in Louisiana and to the events that took place in Bogalusa and in Plaquemines Parish. Because this memoir is my story, based on my reminiscences, it no doubt differs from the experiences and memories of other people who were active in the Louisiana movement from 1966 through 1968. Each of us brought our own personal backgrounds, experiences, perspectives, and goals to the movement. And each of us took from the movement those things that mattered to us—the events, relationships, and interactions with others that helped us to understand, learn, and grow. An incident that only made a fleeting impression on one person may have been a defining moment to another. This memoir is my personal witness. I encourage others in the Louisiana movement to tell their stories, too, before all we have left is history.

THANKS

My heartfelt thanks go out to all of you who contributed, in so many creative ways, to the course of this project. Without your dedicated assistance in editing, researching, and generating ideas, there would have been no book. Most of all, thank you for believing in me.

Kathleen Allenbach, Dahlia Armon, Barrett Black, Maureen and Mike Bowman, Jeff Brand, Erika Büky, Christopher Campbell, Tyrell Collins, John Denvir, Lolis Elie, Peter Elliston, Sue Heinemann, Robert Hicks, Christopher, Liam, and Colleen Honigsberg, Edith Ho, Gayle Jenkins, Don Juneau, Pelonomi Khumoetsile, Chris King, Michael Millemann, Michael Pitre, Richard Sakai, Naomi Schneider, Helen Sigua, Marilyn Tham, Melinda Thomas, Mary Louise Zernicke, and the outstanding faculty and administration at the University of San Francisco School of Law.

ONE

From the Subway
to Mississippi

I am sitting on a bench in Jackson Square. It is early morning, and the city is waking up. Already a line has formed at the Madeleine Bakery, kitty-corner from where I am sitting and where just minutes ago I ordered a fresh apricot custard tart, a gooey "Saint Tropez" whipped cream and vanilla thing, and fresh-squeezed orange juice. Breakfast in New Orleans must be rich and sweet. In fact, every meal in New Orleans must be rich and sweet, or why bother eating? It is not the town for a breakfast of eggs, bacon, and toast or flat, unflavored pancakes. The food here is deep-fried or prepared with cream, sugar, and butter—often a pound of butter per recipe for six.

Beyond the perimeter of the park several quick-sketch portrait artists, along with tarot and palm readers, are setting up their stands to the rhythm of a steel-guitar player banging out the blues. A black man wearing a yellow cap and a green shirt, imprinted with the words "Parkway and Park Commission," skillfully guides his metal rubbish picker to pluck cigarette butts and two tissues squeezed behind my bench. About twenty yards away, a bronzed Andrew Jackson on a rearing horse tips his hat to passersby. The pink and lavender petunias, the unevenly cut lawns, and the cast-iron fences surround him, as they do me. Behind me rises Saint Louis Cathedral, a monument to the French heritage of

New Orleans, its graceful silhouette overshadowing the park and the Mississippi River. I cannot see the Mississippi from my vantage point; years ago the city built a retaining wall running along the river through the Vieux Carré, the French Quarter. But I can observe the Café Du Monde alongside the retaining wall as it begins to fill with tourists who have found the best bargain in town: three beignets—square-shaped donuts deep-fried in brick-colored lard and liberally sprinkled with powdered sugar—and a cup of cafe au lait, a blend of coffee and chicory with milk. The cost: two dollars and twenty cents.

It is overcast; it has been that way all week. But it is springtime, and although the radio is predicting rain and the air is sweaty and laden with the smells and salt of the Gulf, no one seems to mind. For there is no place quite like New Orleans for food, drink, music (Louis Armstrong, the Neville Brothers, Dr. John, Irma Thomas, and the Marsalis family, to name a few homegrown musicians), and downright funk. And as I sit on this park bench, I recall the hot, muggy summer thirty years ago when I walked through the French Quarter each morning on my way to work as a law-student civil rights worker at the Lawyers Constitutional Defense Committee.

It all started in early June of 1966 when, as a first-year law student, I said good-bye to my tearful mother by the entrance to the Fort Tryon Park subway station at the uppermost tip of Manhattan, rode the A train downtown, and boarded a Greyhound bus heading south. I can only imagine what she, a refugee from Nazi-occupied Austria, thought as I boarded that train to join the fight for other people's freedom. We had walked in silence.

The bus stopped at many Southern ports of call—Richmond, Charlotte, Atlanta, Tuscaloosa—places that teased me into the Southern culture. But my destination was Mississippi, the embodiment of all that was wrong with race relations in our country. In reality, Mississippi was not notably more racist than many other places in the South. What I saw and experienced in Louisiana was certainly as unnerving as anything the media portrayed in Mississippi. But Mississippi steadfastly and self-righteously presented itself to the media and to the national consciousness as the last bastion of the Confederacy, the state that would *never* yield to equality among the races. The Mississippi Southern "way of life" would forever resist outside agitators, Commies, and the federal government.

Perhaps that is why the Law Students Civil Rights Research Council chose Jackson, Mississippi, as the location for its summer orientation session. Forty law students from around the country assembled in Jackson that summer. But for nearly all of us, Jackson was merely a transit stop. I was assigned to the New Orleans office of the Lawyers Constitutional Defense Committee. It was from there that I began my odyssey as a legal worker in the Louisiana civil rights movement.

Over the next two years, as I commuted between law school and the South, the essence of my journey became less and less one of destination. In crossing one borderline after another, and in watching and feeling the world change, I changed too. From my initial belief that the issue of black and white relations was a problem that could be solved easily if everyone simply did the right thing, I came to the painful realization that the issue was complex and multilayered, a problem I could no longer understand, much less resolve. As I came to perceive this dilemma, I also understood that the real journey I had been making was not a journey to the South as much as a journey of self-discovery—a soul journey.

That journey of self-discovery, of course, had begun years before, and it continues today. But in examining my formative years, I cannot with any assurance explain what it was that motivated me to go south. My early years as a child of immigrant parents were relatively uneventful, politically and otherwise. Although my parents voted the Democratic party line, I cannot remember their ever voicing a political opinion.

Both my parents fled Austria in 1939 to escape the Nazis. All four of my grandparents died in concentration camps. My father was in his early thirties, my mother in her late twenties when they arrived in the United States with only a high-school education and no knowledge of English.

My father had opportunities in the chocolate and cookie manufacturing trades, but I think he felt that starting his own business was too much of a risk with a young family to support. So he chose the security of a regular paycheck by working in a costume jewelry factory. Later on, when my sister was in high school and I was in college, he realized his dream of owning his own business and purchased a candy store. But whether he worked in the factory or the store, I hardly saw him. He left for work by six in the morning and came home at nine or ten at night. My parents were religious; they observed the Sabbath and kept a kosher home. They often spoke German to me when I was growing up, but, like many first-generation immigrant children, I resisted identifying with their old-world ancestry and refused to speak anything but English.

I can imagine that my mother was embarrassed that her son was going to work in the South. It just wasn't what kids in the neighborhood did, and my mother found her security in a conventional belief system. She had wanted something else for me. I was joining the struggle of a people my German-speaking mother knew as "Schwartzes" and who seemed outside her comprehension and understanding. I am certain she told none of her friends what I was doing.

Before my senior year in college, I was not particularly political. I attended the City College of New York (CCNY), a school that accepted students on the basis of grades alone and that drew its population from the New York boroughs. City College was in upper Harlem, a short bus ride from my home in Washington Heights. The CCNY students and professors projected a passionate belief in justice that dated back to the Depression era of the 1930s. During the fall of 1964 I joined my first protest activities: teach-ins against the Vietnam War. I was inspired, and from then on I was involved in the protest movement.

The next summer I withdrew some of my savings, from jobs I worked during high school and college, and traveled through Europe. But in riding the trains from one country to another, I kept falling into arguments about the war in Vietnam. When I needed to travel through Germany, I was determined to tour the only place that to me was representative of the country—the former concentration camp at Dachau. I was becoming an intense young man.

When I came home from Europe in the fall of 1965, I returned to the familiar and provincial by entering the New York University (NYU) School of Law. Several other law students in my entering class also had activist leanings, and we bonded quickly. In our first month of school we staged a sit-in inside the front hallway to protest the law school dress code, which required that all students wear business dress. Later that school year a law-student civil rights group posted a notice asking for students to work in the South. I volunteered.

By joining in the summer of 1966, I came relatively late to the modern civil rights movement. Many of the milestones of the movement had been passed. I was only sixteen in February 1960, when four freshmen at a black college in Greensboro, North Carolina, held a sit-in at the local Woolworth's lunch counter to demand service for black patrons.[1] In the spring of 1961, when black and white "freedom riders" boarded two Greyhound buses in Washington, D.C., to test the desegregation of interstate transportation in the South, they were viciously bloodied and beaten by mobs in Alabama.

In 1963 Martin Luther King marched on Washington, inspiring many of us with his visionary oration, "I Have a Dream." But within three weeks of his speech, the dream turned into a nightmare when the Ku Klux Klan set off dynamite beneath the Sixteenth Street Baptist Church in Birmingham, Alabama, killing four young girls who were dressing for Sunday morning services.

In 1964 the Council of Federated Organizations (COFO) initiated a program called Mississippi Summer Project/Freedom Summer to assist in voter registration drives and in opening "freedom schools."*

---

* COFO was a loose coalition of members of the National Association for the Advancement of Colored People (NAACP); the Southern Christian Leadership Conference (SCLC), Martin Luther King's organization; the Congress of Racial Equality (CORE); and the Student Nonviolent Coordinating Committee (SNCC). SNCC played the dominant role, followed by CORE.

Hundreds of students from around the country traveled to Mississippi to live in rural communities and offer their assistance. Late one night three civil rights project workers—Michael Schwerner, James Chaney, and Andrew Goodman—were stopped by local sheriff's deputies on a lonely road near Philadelphia, Mississippi, taken to an earthen dam outside town, and summarily executed. Their bodies were buried under tons of Mississippi red clay.

Why didn't I join the college students that summer? I've thought about it many times, and my guess is that it was too early for me to step out of my protected New York environment and venture into the unknown. Besides, I was probably too focused on finding time to be with my girlfriend.

After Freedom Summer, in March 1965, on what has become infamously known as "Bloody Sunday," we all watched the television newscasts in horror as Alabama state troopers and county deputies, swinging clubs and bullwhips, brutally attacked John Lewis, Hosea Williams, and others as they marched from Selma to Montgomery. By the time I arrived in the South in 1966, the movement—symbolized by the circular pin I religiously wore, depicting white and black hands clasped together over a dovetailing black and white background—was changing. I closed my eyes to the changes. I was too new and too committed to civil rights to want to admit that maybe I was on the downside of the movement. I was able to maintain my state of denial for some time, since Louisiana lingered behind Mississippi in acknowledging the changes. But the seeds of change were planted, and the movement was ending. Many people believed that with the passage of the Civil Rights Act of 1964 and the Voting Rights Act of 1965 we had "won"; Black Power, whose tenet of self-determination implied that whites were no longer necessary or even wanted, was on the rise; and people were ready to move on and confront other urgent issues such as the escalating Vietnam War.

Because the movement in Louisiana trailed behind the struggle in Mississippi, I did not need to confront Black Power and its message of exclusion of white activists until 1967. The movement in Mississippi was led by the Student Nonviolent Coordinating Committee (SNCC).[2] Its leaders, Stokely Carmichael and H. Rap Brown, fervently championed Black Power. In Louisiana, however, since the early 1960s sit-ins and boycotts in New Orleans and Baton Rouge, the movement had been closely aligned with the Congress of Racial Equality (CORE).[3] James Farmer, CORE's national director, did not subscribe to the separatist stance advanced by SNCC. CORE officials and workers, as well as African Americans in Louisiana's cities and towns, still welcomed white civil rights legal workers as allies in their drive for equality.

As did most civil rights workers who came down South in the sixties, I carried with me a rather unsophisticated, if not downright simplistic, model of race relations. I saw the movement in stark black and white terms. We were doing God's work, we were on the side of the angels. We were changing the world.

By 1968, I knew differently. By experiencing firsthand the black rural culture of Louisiana as well as the rise of Black Power, I learned how uninformed and unaware my New York City Jewish upbringing had left me. Today, an African American friend laughs at my 1968 realization that racial issues were complex. She points out that race has always been a tangled issue; but until the late sixties, whites did not need to bother about it. When I left the South in 1968, I tried to leave the race problem behind and escape into the anti–Vietnam War movement. Yet I couldn't move away from it, and today, thirty years later, I am still caught up in the complexities of race in America.

At the end of the century, I am still drawn to that idealistic image of the partnership that I experienced while working with the black community in Louisiana. We Northern whites were dramatically different from Southern blacks in our cultures, levels of education, and perceptions of the world. But we all shared a vision of racial justice and equality, and that vision bound us together. Side by side—the local African American community in charge of tactics, the lawyers in charge of litigation— we took personal responsibility for social change. And it worked. The black community became empowered. We created a profound social revolution. Things will never be the same. Nonetheless, much more needs to be done, and my hope is for a renewed partnership in pursuit of social justice.

In writing this memoir, I have tried not to put a nineties spin on a sixties experience. I was a young man in his early twenties who knew very little about anything, especially about race relations. You may find this law student naive and perhaps even self-righteous; I can laugh at him as I read this story over. But I hope you find him true.

When I got off the bus in Jackson, Mississippi, I had no idea what to expect. Since my personal orientation was decidedly urban, I was startled to find that Jackson, the biggest "city" in Mississippi, in no way resembled the city of New York. With a population of about 150,000, 40 percent of which was black, and its lack of any visible financial backbone, Jackson was to me as far from New York as the moon from the earth. With its run-down clapboard houses, greasy taverns, and whitewashed shops, Jackson was small town. And not the kind of small town that I had read about as a kid. This was Deep South small town: red clay walkways alternating with boarded walkways, homes draped with drooping willows and shielded by fragrant honeysuckle, the air dense in furnaced heat layered with drenching humidity, and thick, slow, drawling accents alternating from gracious greetings to hostile contempt if the local whites figured out who you were.

Yet as alien as the communities and neighborhoods of Jackson, Mississippi, had seemed to me that day, nothing prepared me for what I saw the following day. Our group of law students was driven by the local movement people to Mt. Beulah, the site of an old school in the town of Edwards, west of Jackson. The landscape was lined with Quonset huts and wooden-framed shanties. A few of the buildings were set on cement blocks; the others sat directly on the red Mississippi dirt. Dilapidated porches, torn screens, and cross-patched roofs were evident everywhere. There were no paved roads, only dirt roads and walkways. We were told that the blacks who lived here had formerly been tenants on rural plantations but had been evicted by their white landlords for exercising their rights to vote and sending their children to the all-white schools.

As I gaped at these hovels, I thought, "This is why I am here." Earnestly I said to myself, "This is what we must change. And we will. With the law on our side we will overcome the centuries of racism and inequality and make things right." I may have been a fool to think that social forces could be changed overnight, but, God knows, fools were what was needed if anything was ever going to change.

All the law students had been chosen the previous spring to be part of the summer intern program administered by the New York–based Law Students Civil Rights Research Council (LSCRRC), which was started in 1962 to assist civil rights attorneys working in the South. Over the years, as it expanded, LSCRRC also sent law students into Northern communities (which indeed had their share of racism). LSCRRC paid our housing costs and provided us with a minimal stipend.

After the orientation, we were assigned to work with movement lawyers, civil rights legal organizations, and community groups throughout the South. Arrangements had been made for us to be sent to Georgia, Alabama, Arkansas, Virginia, Florida, North Carolina, Texas, Louisiana, and, of course, Mississippi. The largest number of students were sent to Mississippi—perhaps because Mississippi, justifiably or not, was seen as the embodiment of racist Southern culture. The civil rights movement had always focused its limited resources on this state. A few students were assigned to Jackson, but the majority were assigned to rural counties in the Mississippi Delta.

Marian Wright was a young African American lawyer who, soon after graduating from Yale Law School, became the director of the NAACP Legal Defense and Educational Fund (Inc. Fund) office in Jackson.* She greeted us eloquently at the orientation. Her office had been working

* Today, Marian Wright Edelman is the director of the Children's Defense Fund in Washington, D.C.

on school desegregation, challenges to welfare and food-stamp regulations, and voting rights cases on behalf of African Americans in Mississippi. She began by initiating us into the culture we were entering, a culture that to many of us was as foreign as that of any Third World country. No matter how well educated we were and how "uneducated" the people whom we would be assisting, she reminded us, we were to treat every black man, woman, and child with the utmost respect and dignity. We were not to harbor feelings of superiority or allow our egos to blind our vision. She told us that black people in the South risked their jobs and often their lives and the lives of their children every day. At the end of the summer we would be going home, but the people we were helping would still be here. The dust we raised might not have time to settle on us, but it surely would settle on the local black community. After we students returned to school and were no longer around to witness events, the local white population could exact its revenge on the blacks who dared to assert their rights. Things were not always as they seemed, and people could get hurt if we were not careful.

Maintaining Marian Wright's cautionary tone, D'Army Bailey, who had also attended Yale Law School and was LSCRRC's Southern coordinator, explained that the white assault on the black race was becoming more violent in some communities.* This increased white hostility was the result of blacks asserting themselves by sending their children to previously all-white schools; by no longer looking at the ground and murmuring "yessir" when addressing whites; and by marching to the courthouse and registering to vote. The blacks living at Mt. Beulah were a testament to the white resistance to change. Moreover, Bailey added, many of the local white leaders and their supporters believed that African Americans were aligning themselves with "outside agitators" and

---

* D'Army Bailey was instrumental in converting the Lorraine Motel in Memphis, where Martin Luther King Jr. was assassinated, into the National Civil Rights Museum.

"Communists," people who could not understand the "unique relation-ship" that blacks and whites had had in the South prior to the civil rights movement. Blacks might have been "boys" to the Southern white "man," but the tenet of the Southern racist was that as long as the boys "knew their place" there would be no trouble, and the boys would be taken care of. The outside agitators, "nigger lovers," and "Commies" were fomenting trouble, and to the local white racists they were no better than the blacks who listened to them.

D'Army Bailey's unflattering description of the white Southern cul-ture was commonplace. We in the movement did what people have always done: we stereotyped our enemies. By generalizing about the white Southern culture and setting it up as a monolithic evil, the civil rights movement was able to inspire and unite us all to action. By pe-joratively labeling Southern whites as crackers, rednecks, or white trash, we made it easier to rally the troops against a faceless, one-dimensional enemy. (Of course, the Southern whites who depicted us as Commies, nigger lovers, and outside agitators similarly painted us with a superficial and stereotypical brush.)

As with any generalization, stereotyping the Southern culture was misleading. There were many well-intentioned whites who helped move civil rights along. But, unfortunately, they were in the minority. A large segment of white Southern society resisted the change: this was the segment that elected politicians like Alabama governor George Wallace, who proclaimed in his 1963 inaugural address, "Segregation now, seg-regation tomorrow, segregation forever." Had there been enough whites in the South who truly believed in equality and were willing to desegregate the schools, integrate public accommodations, and assure African Americans of their voting rights, there would have been no need for a civil rights movement.

In closing his address, Bailey unceremoniously laid it on the line: if we could not accept direction by members of the African American community, we should "leave tomorrow and return home to confront

[our] own racism." Unita Blackwell, who grew up working in the cotton fields in Mississippi and became a spirited and bold SNCC community organizer, set out the parameters of our jobs.* Trust was an important part of the movement's credo, she observed. So was caution. We were required to inform another person of our whereabouts and the time we expected to be back. If we were not back on time, the black citizenry would send out a search party, and that effort would divert considerable resources. She closed by instructing us not to take the movement lightly. Too many lives, including lives of people we could not know, were at stake.[4]

Next came Henry Aronson, an intense, combative, and feisty white attorney. "I'm going to tell it like it is," he said. Like Marian Wright, he worked for the Inc. Fund. Aronson warned us that our education and social status could not compensate for our probable grave inability to grasp the complexities of Southern black culture. Humility would go a long way in making our tours worthwhile. He also cautioned us to beware of government agencies like the Department of Health, Education, and Welfare (HEW), the Department of Justice, and the FBI. HEW would not always act to enforce the federal school integration guidelines. The Justice Department had a political agenda, he said, because the government did not want to alienate Southern members of Congress.

As for the FBI, Aronson made it abundantly clear that under J. Edgar Hoover the FBI would do no more than "observe" and possibly investigate racially motivated incidents. At best, civil rights workers could regard FBI agents as fact-finders who would report their investigations to the Justice Department. The agents were instructed not to participate directly or interfere in any local police actions, even in situations where the police were themselves harassing or intimidating protesters. Moreover, the FBI was reported to have spies in our organizations as well as

* In the late seventies Unita Blackwell became the first African American woman mayor of Mayersville, Mississippi, a tiny, serene town along the Mississippi River.

in other "subversive" organizations such as the Ku Klux Klan.* Finally, it was very likely that FBI agents reported our impending demonstrations, boycotts, and protests to the local and state governments. Paranoid or not, Henry Aronson concluded, we should never rely on the FBI to protect us.[5]

D'Army Bailey then returned to tell a story that had been creating a buzz among law students that year. It concerned one of the law students who had worked in Mississippi the previous summer. Oliver Rosengart, who was one year ahead of me at NYU School of Law and grew up a block away from me in Washington Heights, was canvassing local blacks in a rural Mississippi community, encouraging them to register to vote. His efforts enraged one of the locals, who took his rifle down from the back of his pickup and aimed it at Ollie outside the voter registration office. Ollie ran and hid behind the cars. The gunman walked all around looking for him, but fortunately he was too drunk to aim straight, and once he ran out of bullets Ollie raced to his car and sped away. But, as D'Army Bailey emphasized, Ollie did not board the next bus back to New York; he saw out the summer in the Mississippi Delta county, continuing to register voters.

During the two-day orientation the leaders took us through various role-playing exercises in which we practiced handling typical encounters with the local white communities and law enforcement agencies. We were instructed not to try to be heroes or martyrs, but just do our jobs and not put ourselves or others in harm's way. Fully "oriented" and humbled, we were sent on our way—to lawyers and community groups in the Mississippi Delta, in the Black Belt of Alabama, in southwest Georgia, in urban and rural Louisiana, and elsewhere in the South.

---

* The FBI maintained a counterintelligence program named COINTELPRO to spy on and infiltrate constitutionally protected organizations. Among the groups that the FBI targeted were CORE, SNCC, SCLC, and the Deacons for Defense and Justice, whose centers of power were in Bogalusa, Louisiana (where I worked), and Jonesboro, Louisiana. See Clayborne Carson, *In Struggle: SNCC and the Black Awakening of the 1960s* (Cambridge: Harvard University Press, 1981).

I'd like to think that we all learned something in that time about ourselves and how we saw the world. Coming from New York, where education and status were the defining factors in my life, my attitudes were very different from the values in which the speakers instructed us. Although the leaders' addresses did not sink in completely during the orientation, I did replay the words over and over again as I watched the African American community in Bogalusa, Louisiana, direct the boy-cotts, the demonstrations, and the integration of public accommodations, while we civil rights workers played our appropriate secondary, yet necessary, roles.

I was assigned to the Lawyers Constitutional Defense Committee (LCDC) office in New Orleans, one of the three legal organizations working for civil rights in the South. LCDC was formed in 1964. Until then there had been two civil rights legal organizations: the recently formed Lawyers' Committee for Civil Rights under Law and the NAACP Legal Defense and Educational Fund.* The Lawyers' Committee had been created a year earlier when President Kennedy re-quested members of the American Bar Association and the private bar to assist the civil rights movement in the South. But in 1964 the Lawyers' Committee, not wishing to antagonize Southern bar associations, took a conservative position and steered clear of direct representation of civil rights workers who were arrested and jailed.

The oldest civil rights legal organization was the NAACP Legal Defense and Educational Fund, or the Inc. Fund.† Through the work of Charles Houston and Thurgood Marshall, the Inc. Fund relentlessly pursued school desegregation cases in federal court.[6] In 1954, Houston's

---

* Initially the Lawyers' Committee was called the President's Committee.
† At one time, the Inc. Fund was part of the NAACP. However, as the objectives of the NAACP and the Inc. Fund diverged during the 1950s and 1960s, the two or-ganizations formally severed their ties. For a detailed account of the split as well as of the inner workings and successes of the Inc. Fund, see Jack Greenberg, *Crusaders in the Courts* (New York: Basic Books, 1994).

and Marshall's dreams were realized. In the renowned U.S. Supreme Court case of *Brown v Board of Education*, Chief Justice Earl Warren, writing for the unanimous court, outlawed state-sanctioned segregation. The euphemism "separate but equal," used for more than fifty years to humiliate African Americans by restricting them to segregated and sub-standard schooling and public accommodations, was withdrawn from the national vocabulary.

In barring segregation in public facilities, the *Brown* decision helped pave the way for the 1960s civil rights movement. However, the Inc. Fund saw its role to be that of initiating major integration test cases, and, after 1954, of implementing the *Brown* decision. Unless larger constitutional issues were at stake, the Inc. Fund would not use its resources to defend individuals from criminal prosecution related to civil rights actions.[7]

In the winter of 1964, as civil rights organizations were preparing for Freedom Summer, it became obvious that the hundreds of students (mostly college students) who were to converge on the South would need legal support. If the Lawyers' Committee and the Inc. Fund would not represent civil rights workers, someone else would have to do it. Certainly the organizations planning Freedom Summer could not rely on local counsel. There were very few black attorneys in the South, and the handful of Southern white attorneys who were sympathetic to the movement feared for their lives and their livelihoods if they defended civil rights workers.

In-house lawyers and directors of the American Civil Liberties Union (ACLU), the National Council of Churches, the Inc. Fund, CORE, the American Jewish Congress, and the American Jewish Committee met the challenge.[8] They agreed to help set up an alternative organization to provide volunteer legal support for the civil rights workers in the South in the summer of 1964. The organizing committee also saw a secondary purpose in sending volunteer attorneys to assist in the Southern movement: they hoped that after their involvement with the movement, the volunteers would continue to perform good works and spread the word to others in their own firms and communities. And so the Lawyers Constitutional Defense Committee was born.[9]

In LCDC's first year of operation, all the sponsoring organizations contributed seed money, with the ACLU and the National Council of Churches providing $15,000 each.[10] In subsequent years, the ACLU absorbed LCDC and became accountable for its funding.

LCDC's organizing committee solicited volunteer lawyers for two- to three-week tours in the South. But by the end of the summer, the committee realized that a more permanent arrangement was required so that the same lawyers could see civil rights cases through to completion, avoiding the lack of continuity and the inefficiency associated with visiting lawyers who stayed only a few weeks. So LCDC created three full-time staff attorney positions and requested commitments of a month or longer from the volunteers. By 1965, LCDC had offices in New Orleans; Jackson, Mississippi; and Selma, Alabama.

The morning after the Law Students Civil Rights Research Council orientation ended in Jackson, I boarded a train called the "City of New Orleans." Within hours I was walking up Dryades Street, through one of New Orleans's largely African American neighborhoods, on my way to the LCDC office.

TWO

Armed Escorts

The Lawyers Constitutional Defense Committee office in New Orleans was located at 2209 Dryades Street, a few doors from the corner of Jackson Avenue. Outside, it was a drab, graying, two-story clapboard structure, but inside it was always buzzing. The building was the center of gravity for the Louisiana civil rights movement. The activist African American law firm of Collins, Douglas, and Elie (CD&E) and the local Congress of Racial Equality office shared space on the second floor. Not much happened in the movement in Louisiana without the involvement of CORE and CD&E. In 1960, when the movement to integrate New Orleans took firm hold, CORE students—who had met Robert Collins when he taught at Southern University—asked the newly formed law firm to represent arrested demonstrators. All three lawyers were young: Nils Douglas and Lolis Elie had graduated from law school at Loyola University in New Orleans the previous year, and Robert a half-dozen years earlier. As a result, they related easily to the students. A spirited long-term bond developed between CORE and CD&E out of that representation.[1] Other than representing CORE, CD&E's legal work in the early 1960s was described by Robert Collins as a "ghetto practice," since most middle-class blacks and black businesses hired white lawyers.[2]

According to one report, Dryades Street in the 1950s and early 1960s was the second largest shopping district in the city and popular with black shoppers (although most of the shops were owned by whites).[3] But when I arrived in 1966, the neighborhood consisted of some local eateries, a tiny shoe repair shop, and a funky five-and-dime store, all apparently owned by blacks. The menus of the eateries down the street from the LCDC office were simple but representative of both the times and the community. Near the corner stood a cafe specializing in fried chicken. Across the street was another fried chicken and dumplings establishment. This shop also served greasy hamburgers on white buns dripping with mayonnaise, a custom that seemed bizarre to New Yorkers like me, who never put mayonnaise on any sandwich made with red meat—only ketchup and mustard would do. But "when in Rome. . . ."

Today, thirty years later, the neighborhood has taken on the aspect of a war-torn city. When I drove down Dryades—a section of which was renamed Oretha Castle Haley Boulevard for the former local CORE president and civil rights activist—I passed block after block of gutted, windowless, and boarded-up buildings. I could still see the number 2209 above the door to the old office. But the number and the outer walls are all that remain.*

The primary goals of the civil rights movement never included the improvement of housing or the health of black neighborhoods, although these may have been indirect goals. Revitalizing the inner city became an integral part of Lyndon Johnson's "war on poverty." But after Johnson diverted the nation's resources to the war in Vietnam, urban centers lost their vigor, and urban blight set in. Unfortunately, Oretha Castle Haley Boulevard is not remarkable in its decay. It stands as a grim reminder of the many burned-out inner-city blocks in cities across America.

My first supervisor that summer was Jeremiah Gutman. Jerry had graduated from New York University School of Law in 1949, where he

---

* When I drove down this street in 1997, the 2209 building and two neighboring structures had been razed.

had been editor in chief of the law review. He ran a general practice in New York, but he devoted much of his time to representing cases for the New York Civil Liberties Union. Volunteering in the South fit right into his activist practice. And unlike most Northern lawyers, who came and went within two weeks, Jerry stayed for a month at a time. The movement needed volunteer attorneys like Jerry Gutman not only because of the scarcity of white Southern lawyers willing to assist but also because black attorneys like Robert Collins, Nils Douglas, and Lolis Elie were subjected, like other black leaders, to Klan and local police violence.* Moreover, there were few black attorneys in the Deep South: in the mid-1960s, there were fewer than a dozen black lawyers in all of Louisiana.

Under laws and gentlemen's agreements created decades before, out-of-state attorneys were permitted to represent local defendants in Southern states. The laws varied from state to state. In Mississippi, lawyers could represent local clients if the attorneys were associated with local counsel, unless two Mississippi bar attorneys from different firms challenged an outsider's credentials. In that case, the Mississippi bar association would decide whether the lawyers were "fit" to appear before the state courts. A similar, though not identical, policy existed in Louisiana, where out-of-state attorneys could represent clients as long as the lawyers were associated with local counsel. Since LCDC did not have a member of the Louisiana bar on its staff until Don Juneau joined in February 1967, LCDC associated with CD&E on civil rights cases.

This association worked fine until 1967. Until then, no law official or judge had challenged LCDC's out-of-state attorneys affiliated with CD&E. In the spring of 1967, however, chief staff counsel Richard Sobol was arrested for the illegal practice of law while representing Gary

* Lolis Elie recalls that in 1963 he, Robert Collins, Nils Douglas, CORE national director James Farmer, and local black marchers were attacked by police with cattle prods and tear gas in the town of Plaquemine (Rogers, *Righteous Lives*, 132–33). Though afraid for their lives, Lolis and the others never gave a thought to quitting the cause.

Duncan, a black man, in the bayous of Plaquemines Parish, Louisiana (see chapter 14).

Jerry Gutman knew how to win cases and protect clients, whether in New York or in Louisiana. But he also knew that by leaving Louisiana after the summer, he left many loose ends. LCDC's executive secretary, Henry Schwarzschild,[4] who handled administrative and fund-raising duties in New York, and its chief counsel, Alvin Bronstein, who supervised all LCDC litigation from Jackson, felt the organization needed someone to take the cases through to the finish. Harris David, the one Northerner who worked in New Orleans as the point man, was a very recent law graduate from NYU who did not practice law: from 1964 to summer 1966 he served as one of the first LSCRRC and LCDC interns.* LCDC had to find and fund a full-time, experienced attorney who could prosecute and manage a caseload after the volunteers left.

They found Richard Sobol. At twenty-eight, Richard was ready for a change. After graduating from Columbia Law School, he had clerked for a federal court judge before accepting a position with Arnold and Porter, one of the most prestigious law firms in Washington, D.C. Richard was a tall, dark-complexioned, good-looking man, with angular features and wavy black hair. I don't know whether he came from a well-to-do family, but he certainly carried himself like someone who was comfortably surrounded by money.

In Washington, Richard defended prominent corporate clients in antitrust cases. He soon became disillusioned and bored by the paper-pushing, high-powered legal world. He was restless and wanted, perhaps needed, a place where he could genuinely help others using his superb legal and organizational skills. In 1965 he contacted LCDC and joined the many lawyers who donated three weeks of their vacation to the movement. But for Richard, unlike many others, the three-week period became more than a story to retell to loved ones and friends; it became a mission. How could he continue pushing paper at a staid Washington firm when he could become an "ambulance service,"[5] taking the

---

* Today, Harris David is senior attorney for New Jersey Legal Services.

movement's emergency cases as they rushed upon him? And where else could he single-handedly file consequential and meaningful cases in federal district (trial) court and take his appeals to the court that was at the cutting edge of civil rights litigation, the Fifth Circuit Court of Appeals?

Richard knew he had superb legal skills and expertise—strengths, he believed, that were not necessarily shared by other Northern civil rights attorneys. Whether in antitrust cases in Washington or civil rights cases in Louisiana, the law was an intellectual pursuit for Richard. Lolis Elie described Richard as a "super lawyer. He could read cases and make them dance."[6] Richard Sobol was a lawyer in the best sense of the term. He loved the law and knew how to use it to help others.

The following year, Richard took a leave from his corporate law practice, packed his bags, and, with his wife, Barbara, and their one-year-old son, left for New Orleans. He began his work for LCDC on August 2, 1966, agreeing to stay for one year. But when he became involved in the *Sobol v Perez* case and the U.S. Supreme Court case of *Duncan v Louisiana*, that year stretched to two. The LCDC salary was low, especially compared to his princely fees at Arnold and Porter. But at least now, in the summer of 1966, what Richard did mattered.

Although I did legal work in the LCDC office under Richard Sobol's guidance, many of my LCDC assignments required me to be in Bogalusa, Louisiana, a company town with a population of about 20,000 people, 7,500 of whom were black. Bogalusa is about sixty miles north of New Orleans across Lake Pontchartrain, a tidal lake twenty-four miles wide. The city's white population is largely Anglo-Saxon Protestant. It is a population more typical of neighboring Mississippi than of southern Louisiana, where people are apt to be related to the Creole (an amalgam of French, Spanish, and African influences and breeding) and Cajun (descendants of the French Acadians who had resettled from Canada and who frequently married into the local Spanish and African populations) Catholic communities. Bogalusa is situated on the murky Pearl River at a point where the river forms a boundary between

Louisiana and Mississippi. The town takes its name from *bogue lusa*, a Choctaw term for dark or smoky waters. Founded by the Great Southern Lumber Company at the turn of the century and later purchased by the Gaylord Container Corporation, which ultimately merged with Crown Zellerbach, Bogalusa was the largest municipality in Washington Parish (acknowledging Louisiana's Catholic heritage, counties are known as parishes). But Bogalusa held another, more dubious distinction during the 1960s. It was reputed to have more members of the night-riding, cross-burning, white-sheeted and hooded Knights of the Ku Klux Klan per capita than any other town in the South.

On my drives to Bogalusa I religiously adhered to the safety routines. First, I rented a car. LCDC had few options when it came to unmarked cars. The LCDC car, a rust-brown, wide-bodied Plymouth, was easy for the FBI, the Klan, or anyone else to recognize and monitor. Several law students and lawyers drove their own cars in Louisiana, and, although they often used them when working for LCDC, they needed to be exceptionally cautious. Driving a car with out-of-state plates—especially New York or California plates—would have been the kiss of death outside New Orleans. Renting different vehicles each time seemed the most prudent choice, but even that tactic had us concerned. Although we never had any proof then, rumor had it that the local rental agencies were issued license plates with specific numbers, plates that white racists could instantly recognize. To avoid attracting notice, we rented our cars from the large national agencies, who, we theorized, would be less likely to have developed bonds with the locals; and, at least, the national agencies would have too many cars to keep track of those rented by civil rights workers.*

---

* Calvin Trillin reported that the Mississippi State Sovereignty Commission had paid spies in the Council of Federated Organizations (COFO), the umbrella organization of the Freedom Summer voter registration drive, and that the commission distributed license plate numbers of COFO cars, including the car that Schwerner, Chaney, and Goodman had been driving on the night they were murdered ("State Secrets," *New Yorker*, May 29, 1995, 54).

The second step of my pre-Bogalusa routine was to make a call from a phone booth at the corner of Dryades and Jackson to a number in Bogalusa that belonged to one of the Deacons for Defense and Justice, the first black organization in modern times to arm itself against the Ku Klux Klan. I never called from the LCDC office. We were certain that the New Orleans police and FBI men were tapping LCDC's phone. In times of crisis, when people in Bogalusa were jailed, we could hear all kinds of cacophonies and echoes when we picked up the phone. Sometimes we suspected that the phone booth at the corner was also tapped. Paranoia, not really unjustified, came quickly in those days.

If I had time, which was not all that often, I made a third stop before I left. I took a slight detour down Magazine Street and stopped at Casamento's to pick up a deep-fried oyster po'boy, bathed in mayonnaise and ketchup, on soft French bread. Among locals, Casamento's was the place for oysters, but actually it didn't make much difference where I bought dinner. In New Orleans, no matter where you went to eat, the seafood gumbo, the red beans and rice, the oyster po'boys, the more adventurous crawfish etouffée, and anything else you ordered were fabulous. Any local cafe offered a memorable eating experience.

From New Orleans, I drove across the Lake Pontchartrain Causeway, touted by the state as the "world's longest bridge." It was only two lanes wide then (it has four lanes now), and, except for a handful of brief rises and falls, the causeway rode straight and flat twelve feet above the water. During the many times that fog nestled on the lake, water and sky merged. I would inch along the causeway, first dreading that the car up ahead had halted and that I would soon be upon it, then fearing that I had strayed across the divider and was bound for a head-on collision. I would have liked to lean back, listening to the radio blasting Lee Dorsey's "Working in a Coal Mine," and savor that surreal drive. But as the miles raced past and I drew closer to Bogalusa, I feared an even worse fate than crashing. The fusion of water and sky was only a mild distraction from the stark threat of violence, chases, shootings, and beatings by Klan members should they happen to be waiting.

At the end of the causeway I turned onto Highway 58, drove un-eventfully past the towns of Mandeville and Covington, and crossed over the Honey Island Swamp at Pearl River. The long-leafed, yellow lob-lolly pines hugging the road were a constant reminder of my destination. Loblolly pine, or pulp pine, as it was known among the mill workers, was developed in the early years of the century at Louisiana State University as a source of fast-growing timber for the Bogalusa Paper Mill. The mill has changed ownership several times over the years, but the loblolly pine has served all its masters well.

When I reached the old bridge on the outskirts of Bogalusa, I pulled over to the side of the road and braked. Fearing that one day I might see the wrong color faces waiting for me, I lifted my eyes slowly, scrutinizing the cars waiting ahead. Inevitably I saw them: two late fifties or early sixties models, with distinctive tail fins. Inside each car sat anywhere from four to six black men, ranging in age from twenty to sixty. Some, showing no signs of recognition, faced forward, their rifles pointing straight ahead. Others looked up to greet me but wasted no time in cordialities. The welcoming could wait until I reached relative safety on the other side of Border Street. The Deacons for Defense and Justice had come to meet me and escort me safely into town.

I never drove into town without their escort, and neither did any other civil rights worker. If the Deacons were not waiting, rumor had it that the Klan would be. And if the Klansmen recognized a civil rights worker, they would give chase. Since no civil rights worker wanted to come face to face with Southern racists carrying shotguns, the worker would speed up. Soon he would be forced to drive at ninety or more to stay ahead of the crackers. That was just what the Klan wanted. A panicked civil rights worker could easily lose control on that narrow two-lane blacktop and crash into a ditch, and no one would be the wiser.

While I waited by the road outside Bogalusa, one of the Deacons' cars moved into position in front of my rented car, and the other car pulled in behind. Then, to avoid any possible confrontations with the Klan, we zoomed through the white neighborhoods, smelling the stink of the white smoke belching from the Crown Zellerbach paper mill. We traveled on well-paved roads through the white districts. Ten minutes later, we whisked across Border Street and into another world. We left the paved roads behind, our tires adjusting to the red dirt and gravel. On days when the tropical rains pounded the state, we drove on muddy roads. There were no traffic lights across Border Street, few street lamps, and only a scattering of stop signs. We were now in the black section of Bogalusa.

THREE

Klan Violence
and the Deacons

Within days of arriving at the LCDC office, I learned about the history of the Bogalusa movement and the formation of the Deacons for Defense and Justice. I needed to understand background as well as culture if I was to be effective in assisting LCDC lawyers and the Bogalusa leaders. A shocking part of Bogalusa's history was that the black community had had to obtain injunctions against the Klan and even against the local police forces to bar them from attacking and harming African Americans. But court action was not always enough. The Deacons were formed in response to the white violence.

The Deacons carried guns, carbines, grenades, and other weapons to defend the black community in Bogalusa. Yet the Deacons have never received the publicity or the notoriety that later black armed groups, like the Black Panthers in Alabama and in Oakland, California, did. Some commentators believe that at their peak the Deacons established more than fifty chapters in towns in Louisiana, Mississippi, and Alabama.[1] Their greatest claim to fame, in fact, occurred not in Louisiana but in Mississippi, in 1966. James Meredith, who in 1961 had integrated the University of Mississippi, announced in 1966 that he would "march against fear" along a lonely highway from Memphis, Tennessee, to Jackson, Mississippi. It was not long before someone took a shot at him, wounding him. When people heard, they came from all over to carry on his march. The Deacons from Bogalusa also came—well armed—to protect the marchers.

Jonesboro, a town in northern Louisiana, is regarded as the home of the original Deacons.[2] The Jonesboro Deacons were organized in 1964. According to one account, two members of the Jonesboro Deacons visited Bogalusa on February 21, 1965, to explain the need for an armed neighborhood patrol and for armed escorts for black activists and civil rights workers, since local law enforcement officials would not protect them.[3] However, Robert Hicks, one of the three principal leaders of the Bogalusa movement, told me that he started the Deacons on February 1, 1965, when he organized armed protection for two civil rights workers.[4] Charles Sims, the first president of the Deacons, also takes credit for being part of the group that created the Deacons.*

Whatever its exact origin, the Bogalusa Deacons for Defense and Justice group was formed in response to intimidation, harassment, and beatings of black demonstrators and picketers in the city of Bogalusa and Washington Parish.[5] Klan violence in Bogalusa was so flagrant, and so obviously condoned by the white law enforcement agencies, that only a black armed force like the Deacons could counterbalance it.

Court orders alone could not stem the violence. The LCDC, together with federal Justice Department lawyers, convinced federal

---

* Sims told this to Howell Raines in *My Soul Is Rested* (New York: Putnam, 1977), 417. Robert Hicks contradicts Sims's account by saying that he himself installed Sims as the president of the Deacons in order to get Sims out of the Bogalusa Voters League, the local black political organization. According to Hicks, Sims, a heavy drinker, had become seriously disruptive at meetings and a nuisance, if not a liability, to Hicks and the others in the League. "Electing" Sims president of the Deacons enabled Hicks and the others to keep Sims out of League meetings.

Sims was eventually replaced by the vice president, Royan Burris. Burris owned a barbershop in town, and the Deacons often congregated there. Although Burris worked with all three of the prominent Bogalusa leaders—A. Z. Young, Robert Hicks, and Gayle Jenkins—he was not interested in attracting media attention, especially white media attention, or in commingling with the white civil rights workers. But he was very committed to his role in the community.

judges to issue two separate injunctions. One was directed against the local Klan and its members. The other, appallingly, had to be directed against the local police. Together the injunctions directed the city and parish police and the local Klan to refrain from beating, clubbing, and otherwise harassing or injuring black demonstrators. Yet even these rare federal decrees did not end the violence.

A unique federal court decision against the Klan was issued in December 1965, six months before I arrived in Louisiana. The case, *United States v Original Knights of the Ku Klux Klan*, was brought by the United States Department of Justice.[6] Judge John Minor Wisdom, one of the most courageous judges in the South, wrote the opinion.[7] At the start of his opinion, Judge Wisdom wrote that the Klan, "whether cloaked and hooded as members of the Original Knights of the Ku Klux Klan, or skulking in anonymity as members of a sham organization, 'The Anti-Communist Christian Association,' or brazenly resorting to violence on the open streets of Bogalusa, are a fearful conspiracy against society, holding men silent by the terror of their acts and their power for evil."[8]

Before Judge Wisdom issued his injunction, he held a hearing to gather the facts on Klan harassment and intimidation in the community. The Klan, dreading a protracted hearing and the disapproving publicity it would raise, admitted from the start that its purpose was to prevent blacks in Bogalusa and Washington Parish from exercising their civil and political rights. Klan activities included showing up hooded—a hundred and fifty strong—at a meeting with the mayor, Jesse H. Cutrer Jr., and the public safety commissioner, Arnold D. Spiers. The mayor later admitted that he was "frightened when he looked into 150 pairs of eyes."[9] On other occasions Klansmen brandished clubs and threatened to kill black patrons in a Bogalusa restaurant, threw an ignited gas canister at a group of blacks standing near the Bogalusa Labor Temple, and assaulted two white civil rights workers. Local Klansmen also attacked blacks in a park with bats, belts, and other weapons, passed out wooden clubs to white thugs stationed along the route of black marchers in downtown Bogalusa, and burned crosses at the home of the editor of the Bogalusa newspaper, who was supportive of civil rights actions.

The Klan also printed handbills containing "crude, scurrilous" attacks on prominent Bogalusa citizens who advocated a moderate approach to desegregation. The handbills accused the editor of the local paper, the owner of the local radio station, several religious leaders, and other Bogalusa and Washington Parish community members and officials of betraying the "Southern way of life" and of "selling people out at every turn." They also proclaimed threats. One leaflet read, "The Ku Klux Klan is strongly organized in Bogalusa and throughout Washington and Tammany Parishes. Being a secret organization, we have Klan members in every conceivable business in the area. We will know . . . who did and did not attend [a meeting called by moderates in the community to resolve racial issues]. . . . Those who do attend this meeting will be tagged as integrationists and dealt with accordingly by the Knights of the Ku Klux Klan."[10]

One of the chief—and absurd—arguments of the attorney representing the Klan was that the Klan no longer existed but had been replaced by the Anti-Communist Christian Association. The attorney ludicrously explained to the court the reason for the change: "The Klan had a bad reputation. Every act of violence that was committed any place was put at the door of the Klan. We had to improve our image."[11] Judge Wisdom made short shrift of this contention, finding that indeed the Klan continued to exist under various "benign" names, including the "Anti-Communist Christian Association"[12] and the "Bogalusa Gun Club," and that, in keeping with its secret agenda, the Klan's principal office was in the Disabled American Veterans Hall.

A list of former members of the Original Knights of the Ku Klux Klan made public at the trial included Robert Rester, Bogalusa's city attorney, as well as several auxiliary city police officers. Rester was responsible for prosecuting people arrested for violence against local blacks and civil rights demonstrators.

Despite its severe tone, Judge Wisdom's injunction in December 1965 had little effect in halting or even moderating the Klan's activities. In 1966 and 1967 members of the Klan attacked the first two black deputy sheriffs in the history of Washington Parish, killing one and seriously injuring the other; attempted to burn down a black church; fired into a black church during worship; shot into the car of a black leader's wife; and attempted to murder a black army captain home on leave from Vietnam while he was using a public telephone. In none of these instances was anyone prosecuted, much less convicted.

The court decree enjoining the local law enforcement agencies from beating and clubbing their citizens actually preceded the *Ku Klux Klan* case by six months. In July 1965 federal judge Herbert W. Christenberry issued an injunction against Bogalusa and Washington Parish law enforcement officials, ordering them to halt their beating, clubbing, and harassing of local African Americans. The lawsuit leading to the injunction was filed by Robert Hicks against the chief of police, Claxton Knight, and other city and parish law enforcement officials *(Hicks v Knight)*.[13]

During the early years of the Bogalusa civil rights movement, in 1964 and 1965, the local city and parish law enforcement officials not only had failed to protect demonstrators and picketers from white thugs who attacked and clubbed them but had even participated in the attacks. African Americans who were arrested during protests were routinely and severely beaten by the police who ostensibly "broke up" the fistfights. Black demonstrators and picketers were beaten in city streets and parks, in police cars, and in the jails. Even black children who participated in the demonstrations received no mercy. In one incident in which children were acting as testers to integrate a local park, Robert Hicks's son Gregory, aged fifteen, was bitten by a police dog. The police were supposedly rushing in to break up a fray caused by white gangs attacking the children. Only minutes before the brawl, however, the same white bands had been seen fraternizing with the police just outside the park.

In issuing the injunction against the local police, an irate Judge Christenberry made it clear that he would not tolerate legal disorder and violence among the police organizations in Bogalusa and Washington Parish. Police officers were put under strict orders to protect blacks from harassment and intimidation and to guarantee that they themselves would not participate in any violent actions or otherwise assault or intimidate the blacks in the community.

The concept of a federal court having to order local law enforcement officials to undertake their job and enforce the law to protect citizens was stunning, even to those of us in the movement. We had come to see the police as outlaws during the past few years, owing to such shameful incidents as the killing of Chaney, Schwerner, and Goodman by local sheriffs in Philadelphia, Mississippi, during Freedom Summer 1964 and Sheriff Bull Connor's dogs attacking demonstrators marching with Martin Luther King in Birmingham in 1963. And now the entire police departments of Bogalusa and Washington Parish had to be put on notice to fulfill their duties as state officials and not participate in violence against their own communities.

Unfortunately, Judge Christenberry's injunction had little effect. Within days after he issued his injunction, local law enforcement officials again cavalierly refused to discharge their duties to protect their community. When racists attacked civil rights picketers at a shopping center, the police did not step in until the seventh attack. And when they did intervene, they arrested seven of the picketers for trespassing. One demonstrator who had been beaten nearly unconscious was arrested for disturbing the peace. The next day civil rights marchers, who had been drenched with water hoses while the police looked on, were taken into "protective custody." None of the attackers was arrested, not even one who, while hosing a demonstrator, scrubbed the protester with a bar of soap, saying, "You still smell a little bit like nigger to me."[14]

In October, on a day known as "Bloody Wednesday," as African American demonstrators were marching to the jail to protest the arrests of civil rights leaders earlier that day, police officers apparently ran amok. They indiscriminately clubbed both civil rights demonstrators on their way to the jail and bystanders who had no connection with the movement. The police also dragged blacks out of cars, striking them with nightsticks, and entered African American bars and assaulted the patrons. A city detective was quoted as saying, "We're tired of you niggers trying to take over the town."[15] Gayle Jenkins, one of the three major leaders of the Bogalusa movement and secretary of the Bogalusa Voters League, and Robert Hicks's wife, Valeria, known to everyone as Jack, had expected police violence. They had tried to persuade the marchers to disperse but were unsuccessful.

Judge Christenberry, in listening to the testimony recounting this night of terror and determining whether the injunction had been violated, commented that "this sounds more like East Germany than the United States." In the following days the judge told the law enforcement officers he did not believe their claim that they were breaking up a disturbance. "I think the record shows that this was a deliberate scheme to harass these people, confuse them and throw them in jail, in as wild a manner as possible. . . . It appears now that the police and the sheriff's office are taking up where the citizens left off. They are committing the violence themselves."[16] Outraged, Christenberry also lectured Claxton Knight: "Chief, I want to tell you, as one man to another, if your brand of law enforcement continues in Bogalusa much longer, the people who live there will be identifiable by the scars and lumps on their heads."[17]

Knight, the lead defendant in Robert Hicks's suit against the local and county police departments, retaliated by filing a multimillion-dollar defamation suit against Hicks. As Hicks tells it, Knight's lawsuit lay idly in the clerk's office and was never pursued in litigation. Yet for years, while the suit lay dormant, the local courts placed legal restrictions on Hicks's home, encumbering its sale and limiting his access to his equity and other assets.

It was in this atmosphere that the Deacons for Defense and Justice was born. With no one looking after the safety of the African Americans in Bogalusa, and with the police apparently determined to harm them, they felt had to take care of themselves.

There were contradictory stories about the Deacons' weapons. The carrying of rifles and pistols was common among both whites and blacks throughout the rural South.[18] Reports said that the Deacons carried not only pistols and rifles but also grenades and machine guns.[19] An FBI report on the Deacons found neither grenades nor machine guns in their arsenals.[20] The director of the Louisiana State Police also believed that the Deacons did not carry such weapons.[21] However, when I rode with Charles Sims on an attempt to integrate a beach, I saw an arsenal of grenades and carbines in the trunk of his car.

The Deacons imposed a curfew on the black neighborhoods. Any car driving at night in the neighborhoods had to provide the correct head-light signal to an approaching Deacon car or risk being stopped. When-ever a group of Klansmen or white thugs were foolish enough to drive through Bogalusa's black neighborhoods at night shooting into homes, the Deacons responded by returning fire and forcing the whites to speed back across Border Street. But whether they caught the white hoodlums or not, the Deacons always responded the following night by driving at least two carloads of men through the white neighborhoods and firing into their homes.

Border Street was a busy crossing—especially at night. The police always suspected certain people, both white and black, but never ar-rested anyone. It was tacitly understood that an eye-for-an-eye response was acceptable, especially when the shooting was to intimidate rather than injure. Rarely was anyone hurt in these armed night "patrols," although many blacks were severely injured in other town incidents.

FOUR

First Cousins

After we crossed Border Street, the Deacons usually escorted me to Gayle Jenkins's house. Gayle was secretary of the Bogalusa Voters League. Her home and Robert Hicks's home were the nerve centers of the Bogalusa movement. People from eight to eighty ran in and out, planning, scheming, organizing, phoning, gossiping, and laughing. They strategized about the long-term issues of integrating the labor force and unions at the Crown Zellerbach paper mill and sending their children to the formerly all-white schools under the "freedom of choice" plan; they schemed about the next day's activities, the boycotts, the picketing, the demonstrations, the testing; they organized the children and adults who would participate; they contacted the media to alert them to the action; they phoned Jerry Gutman and Richard Sobol in New Orleans for legal advice and for information on how the Department of Justice and the FBI might become involved. They revisited the day's events, and sometimes the talk melted into tears at news that someone had been injured by white gangs or even by police officers. And through it all, with Gayle leading, they laughed at the follies and foibles of the other side.

Gayle always put me up when I stayed overnight. Just as Gayle's spirited energy and vivaciousness were unmatchable in the community,

so too her home stood out. While nearly everyone's home was of clapboard construction, painted (and often peeling) in shades of white,
green, and gray, Gayle's home was solid red brick. Gayle herself was
thin, with light brown skin, and although she was only of medium height
she seemed to carry herself six feet tall. When I knew her, Gayle was in
her late thirties. Her magnetism held me as it must have held others.
All of us—the African American residents and the white civil rights
workers—looked to her for leadership. And, along with Robert Hicks
and A. Z. Young, she led.

Gayle Jenkins never flinched from her commitment to the community, never retreated from speaking from her heart and standing up to
the white power structure. There were no subtleties. When she spoke,
people, black and white, listened. Almost daily she was on the phone
making demands of the white police chief, sheriff, or mayor. Gayle had
a direct line to Bogalusa's seat of power. And it went both ways: when
city officials sought information or wanted to negotiate an end to a
demonstration, boycott, or strike, they called Gayle. And they called her
often.

In 1965, Gayle was cooking meals at a hospital clinic for $19.20 a
week when her white boss forbade her to leave work early to join the
demonstrations and boycotts of white businesses on Columbia Road,
Bogalusa's main thoroughfare.* "I was supposed to be the good nigger,"
Gayle recalls today as she chain-smokes another cigarette. But on that
day she walked out of the clinic, never to return. For the next two years
she devoted herself full-time to the movement.

The Louisiana governor at the time, John McKeithen, called Gayle
Jenkins "the little radical woman." But in spite of that appellation, or
perhaps because of it, Governor McKeithen offered her a secretarial job
in the state capital at $50,000 a year. As she sees it, the job offer was

---

* Actually, the signs read "Columbia Street," but the locals refer to it as Columbia
Road. As Robert Hicks told me, in the old days you were always "going down the
road."

designed to get her out of Bogalusa. As anyone could have predicted, she turned it down.

Gayle grew up in Bogalusa. Her grandmother had moved with her daughter, Gayle's mother, to Bogalusa from Monticello, Mississippi, at the end of World War I, when her mother was a young girl. Gayle showed me a photo of her mother on the mantel. Her mother looked white to me. Gayle agreed, acknowledging that her mother's father was white. Gayle's mother died at thirty-nine, when Gayle was sixteen. She never knew her father; he died when she was nine months old.

I asked Gayle whether she was ever frightened during the movement. "No, I really wasn't afraid," she told me. "Things happened spontaneously, I didn't have time to think of the consequences. I was constantly doing something. . . . I guess I didn't have sense enough to be afraid." But she continued, "My husband was afraid. And once, when my daughter was at a demonstration and came running into the house saying, 'Mom, the police are down there,' I said to her, 'Go right back down there.'" Gayle didn't know where her courage came from. She remembers her mother as timid. "She wouldn't say nothing, she would have been scared for me," Gayle softly remarked.

At seventy-one, Gayle Jenkins is still making herself heard as a member of the local school board, on which she has served for more than twenty-five years. Her daughter, Toni, is now the principal of an elementary school in Bogalusa. At a Black History Week celebration in the local church in 1998, Robert Hicks described Gayle as the only person in Bogalusa who remained committed throughout her life.

Today, they call Gayle Jenkins "Duracell Battery." "I never give out, day or night," Gayle said to me. "I get up running and go to bed running. Somebody's got to keep going." And although she says that the whites are still looking for the "good nigger," she is not the one. "They don't like me, but they respect me. I know they respect me. . . . I feel free. I ain't got to ask Mr. Jones or Mr. Smith. I *am* Mr. Jones or Mr. Smith. I do what I want to do."

When I asked Gayle whether she would do it again, she said that she "would go the same route," except that she would not integrate the schools. Integrating the schools did not work: the schools added science labs, but lost community, she observed. Back then people *wanted* to go to school. "You make them go now!"

Gayle also says that although she would still fight to integrate restaurants and all public accommodations, integration has had a negative effect on local black businesses. When the white shops became accessible, African Americans switched their trade to white-owned businesses, which provided better goods at lower prices. The African American businesses could not compete. Even today, "We don't have anything to generate money."[1] As Gayle sees it, the only black-owned properties in the Bogalusa community are houses and churches.

In the early 1970s, Gayle Jenkins tried to obtain a Small Business Association loan to build and run a local market down the street from her home. But the government required her husband to cosign the papers. He refused, apparently because he did not want to take the financial risk. Whatever the reason, Gayle was disappointed. She would have been a shrewd businesswoman, and if anyone could have run a successful market in the neighborhood, she would have been the one.

Society has gone backward in other ways too, Gayle believes, though not as far back as it was in her days. We're at a standstill, she reflects. A lot of the people who fought in the movement are dead. "And the younger ones are not thinking about the movement. They are only thinking about standing on the corner and using that crack. . . . It's a hurting thing, after all that struggle you went through."

She laments that kids today have little interest or appreciation of what happened in the 1960s. When Gayle tells her grandchildren stories of the movement, they respond with comments like, "You went through the back door?" "I say 'yeah,' " she answers. "Well, why did you do it?" they ask. "I wouldn't have gone through no back door!"

In a view consistent with her steadfast vision and resolve, Gayle Jenkins is unsentimental about those movement days. I asked her whether she had any old photographs of herself and the movement. She told me

I was too late. Just recently she had taken out all her articles and photos from that time, including a picture of herself from the front page of the *New York Times*, and carried them to the front lawn. Then she lit a match to them. Gayle's eyes are set on the future. She does not look back.

In the summer of 1966, the major protest activity was picketing and boycotting stores on Columbia Road. Adults and children would walk the picket lines every day, rain or shine, demanding that the white shop owners hire blacks in responsible positions. And when it came to violence, Columbia Road was ground zero. Nearly every day, what began as a peaceful demonstration would erupt into a brawl. The boycott hurt the pocketbooks of the white merchants, and tension was high.

Often a simple act started the fray. Perhaps, as happened more than once, it began when a white man dropped a lighted cigarette on the skirt of a black girl picketer and then slipped his hand under the girl's skirt while reaching for his cigarette. Then, as if on cue, other young and middle-aged white thugs, who seemed to have nothing better to do than stand around fraternizing with each other and with the white police officers stationed there to "guard" the demonstrators, would rush in, perhaps chanting words like "jigaboos" and "coons," and attack the black picketers. But the Deacons had their own "observers" on the scene, and when the whites struck, the blacks responded. As if the scene were scripted, the police officials, after assuring themselves that the white bands had caused as much damage as they could and were now under siege by the blacks, would enter the melee and "clear out" the demonstrators by clubbing them and then hauling them off to jail for "disturbing the peace."

Gayle, Bob, and A.Z. always volunteered to be the first arrested, an offer unwelcome to the white authorities. Every time the leaders were arrested, the word spread across Border Street in minutes. Immediately someone in the movement called LCDC in New Orleans. Within a couple of hours I would be driving to Bogalusa to investigate the incident, interview the participants, and prepare affidavits. Armed with these statements attesting to the arrests and the brutality, I returned the next day to New Orleans, where the affidavits were submitted to the federal judges who had issued injunctions in the *Hicks v Knight* and *Ku Klux Klan* cases. And once again we would document that the police and the local Klan were violating the injunctions by assaulting African American citizens.

Gayle and Bob were united not only in protest but also in family. They were first cousins, and at one point in their childhood Gayle had lived at Bob's parents' home. Robert Hicks was lanky and had tender brown eyes. I thought of him then as one of the most decent and compassionate men I had ever known, and thirty years later I feel the same. Bob was always soft-spoken, dignified, and reasonable in his dealings with the more strident Deacon members as well as with the elected officials and other dominant members of the white community. He did not need to raise his voice; his authority was expressed in his thoughtful words and his exemplary conduct. Bob was the inspirational leader, the beloved Nelson Mandela of the Bogalusa movement. He and Gayle always consulted together before deciding on tactics and direction. Never did I see them disagree on goals and objectives. They were a powerful, united team, and the local whites knew it.

Robert Hicks is also the most gracious of men. When I called from New Orleans to ask whether I could visit and interview him, he said that he would indeed be at home. "I'm always around, I'm retired," he chuckled. He invited me to join him and his wife, Jack, for breakfast and coffee. Bob and Jack live in a modest, two-story brick and wood-siding home, set back from a main road. But their wall hangings are definitely not average. Tacked above the couch in the living room are four eight-sided signs. They read "Stop David Duke, Vote Nov. 16th." (Duke, a former grand wizard of the Ku Klux Klan, made a forceful bid for the Louisiana governorship in 1991.)

Born in a small Mississippi town near Hattiesburg, Bob moved to Bogalusa with his family when he was two. In Mississippi, his father had logged swamps, using oxen to pull out the stumps. But he fell on hard times, and after relocating his family to Bogalusa he became a share-cropper. In those years Bogalusa was called the "Magic City" and was the fastest-growing community in Louisiana. The local paper mill attracted workers and other businesses, making Bogalusa the sixth largest city in the state. (Today, perhaps largely because no major thoroughfare runs through Bogalusa, many other cities have surpassed it in size.)

In January 1965, as treasurer of the Bogalusa Voters League, Bob watched in frustration as white officials deceived the black community on an agreement to integrate local businesses. Believing that CORE's intervention was needed to assist the movement, Bob offered to take into his home two white members of CORE.[2] By doing so, Bob provoked the Klan, targeting himself and his family for retaliation.

Lolis Elie regards Bob as the bravest person in the Bogalusa struggle.[3] In fact, had it not been for the Deacons for Defense—who drove Bob to and from work at the local Crown Zellerbach paper mill, accompanied him on his breaks, and sat with him in the shower room until he was ready to leave—Bob would likely have been killed.*

Bob once held the lowest-paying job at the paper mill, but when Crown felt pressure to elevate one of its African American employees to a supervisory position, overseeing both blacks and whites, it chose Bob Hicks to be the first black foreman. Bob held that position until he retired nearly twenty years later. At one point Crown offered him a job at its offices in San Francisco. Guessing that it wanted to maneuver him out of town, he refused, just as Gayle Jenkins had declined the governor's job offer. Today Jack and Bob, aged sixty-eight, own more than a dozen houses in Bogalusa, guaranteeing a secure retirement.

Looking back thirty years, Bob reflects that in hindsight he would have done things differently—"a lot differently."[4] He would have established himself as more of a public figure—put himself squarely into

---

* Today, the Crown Zellerbach paper mill is owned by Gaylord, the company that started the mill in the early 1920s. Gaylord sold the mill to Crown in the 1960s and repurchased it in the 1980s.

the limelight and not "let anybody come in and take over." Bob feels that people today do not fully appreciate and credit him for all he gave to the Bogalusa movement.

During my interview with Bob, he told me that he too was planning to write a book. He had several options. A screenwriter from New York was pursuing him to coauthor a story about the Deacons for Defense. But Bob was concerned about the emphasis of such a screenplay. "I don't want another *Mississippi Burning*," Bob said to me, referring to a film widely criticized for giving undeserved credit to the FBI for its role in the civil rights struggle. Eventually, the film negotiations collapsed.

Bob understood the conflict between encouraging many people to document their experiences of Bogalusa's civil rights history and the fact that too many versions might result in a distortion of the facts. He acknowledged that all of history "depends on different people's points of view [and that] no one has sole monopoly" on the story. But then, perhaps alluding to me, he observed that someone "who just went to meetings and marches but did not make decisions could also think, 'I was a principal player and I want to write on it.' " Emphasizing this point, Bob concluded, "If the story is to be told, it's got to be told by a principal player of the movement."

Bob has an important story to tell. So does Gayle Jenkins, although she has said to me that she has no intention of writing her story; she is too busy carrying on the cause. A.Z. Young, the third principal player and the former president of the Bogalusa Voters League, is dead. His story can only be told by others. Jack Hicks told me that one day she, Bob, and their five children will sit down before a tape recorder and record everyone's memories of those times.[5] I hope they do. But in the meantime none of us is getting any younger. And my story, albeit a story from a foot soldier, may be for the moment the only firsthand perspective on the Bogalusa civil rights movement and its spirited grass-roots leaders.

In reflecting that other people's versions of his story will not be the same as his own, Robert Hicks is also suggesting something else. Today,

Bob grasps what he did not understand thirty years ago: that the events of that time changed the country forever. And he now understands that when he chose to stay in the background and allow A. Z. Young to take the glory before the television cameras and the newspaper reporters, Bob secured himself a permanent back seat on the bus to prominence. For it is the name of A. Z. Young, not Robert Hicks, that people in Louisiana immediately associate with the Bogalusa civil rights movement.*

For me the events in Bogalusa were very exciting at first. But it did not take long before I became restless watching Bob, Gayle, A. Z., and the others placing their lives and bodies on the line every day while I just gathered facts and listened to their stories in the evenings. And as I became restless, I became more thoughtful. If being a lawyer meant just standing apart watching others, was that what I really wanted to do? I shuddered to think of a lifetime of envying others in action while I stood on the sidelines taking notes, drafting affidavits, and writing briefs.

Not long after I saw myself in this quandary, I had my first chance to be a part of the action. I was invited to join a mixed group of local blacks and white CORE members to test integration at the Acme Cafe on Columbia Road, which was known to be sympathetic to the Klan. There were five of us: Gayle Jenkins; Gayle's niece; a young member of the Deacons; Tyrell Collins, a white CORE worker from California who lived in Bogalusa that summer; and me. We met at Gayle's house. Before we left, we let Robert Hicks know where we were going. If we did not return by a certain time, he and others would look for us. They were to begin by checking both the city and county jails and then call Jerry Gutman in New Orleans.

Gayle drove. We reached the Acme Cafe, parked, and walked in. No one came to seat us, so we took an empty table. The other white cus-

---

* Of course, if Bob had acted with an eye toward the future, he might have conducted himself differently and perhaps not as effectively.

tomers—there were no black patrons—halted their conversation to stare at us. I can still see a middle-aged woman's eyes glowering at us from the neighboring table. She looked like a woman who in other circumstances probably could have been charming. I noticed a white middle-aged man get up from another table and leave the restaurant. Then another, younger man rose and went to the phone booth.

Never having been a tester before, and never having trained as one, unlike the CORE workers who lived in Bogalusa, I had no idea what was expected of me or what might happen. Nor did I know what to do if we were arrested for some trumped-up charge, or, even worse, attacked by Klan members or the police.

For about twenty minutes we just sat there. No one said a word to us, including the gum-chewing teenage waitress. Finally, Gayle called out for service. The waitress took her time to arrive at our table. She passed menus out to the African Americans at the table. "Under the Civil Rights Act, I have to serve you niggers," she said. Then, eyeing Tyrell and me, she sneered, "But I don't have to serve you two who are even worse than niggers. You're nigger lovers."

Gayle said that she would like an ice cream shake. The other two black members in our party asked for the same. Tyrell and I did not even try to order. In one way, I found the waitress's literal interpretation of the law amusing. Of course she had to serve all her customers, not just the black patrons. But I was in no mood to laugh. I was incredibly unsure what constituted appropriate behavior, if such there was in these situations. I didn't want to make a scene and cause injury to the others. Besides, I kept flashing on the actions of the two white men who had left. Tyrell too sat quietly.

The waitress brought the three shakes fifteen minutes later. Just as Gayle and her two friends were about to begin sipping their drinks, a Deacon who, unknown to us, had been positioned outside the cafe came rushing to our table. "Let's go," he shouted. "Quickly! They're calling for reserves. Some have arrived already."

I looked out the door. Several white men were clustering a few yards away on the sidewalk. We all headed for the door. I cannot remember whether anyone left money for the bill. We jumped into the car and took off. Two souped-up 1960s Oldsmobiles filled with white men drove up as we left. I noticed a Deacons' Chevy driving close behind us. In our car no one said a word.

It wasn't until we returned to Gayle's place that I was able to relax. We all needed to release the pent-up tension. Gayle stood up and imitated the waitress: "Service for niggers but not for nigger lovers." We loved telling and retelling the story and even acting it out for everyone who came through the door. By the end of the evening, the entire community knew about the episode. How exhilarated we were. Emotions swept high and dipped low from day to day. That day was a high on the other side of Border Street.

I relived that day at the Acme Cafe again and again, and I wanted more. I loved the action, the thrill. I was aware of the perils—you couldn't ignore them when people were beaten every day—but somehow I felt secure in knowing that the Deacons were nearby. Besides, the adventure was worth the risks. It was a lot more exciting than collecting affidavits.

FIVE

Evenings at Cozy Corners

On evenings when I stayed over in Bogalusa, I often attended Bogalusa Voters League (BVL) planning and strategy sessions at the Ebenezer Baptist Church or at the union hall. If there was no need for a formal meeting, we gathered at Cozy Corners, a pool hall and tavern down the street from Gayle Jenkins's home in Poplas Quarters (Poplas had been a Greek landowner). A. Z. Young managed Cozy Corners.

It was not much of a pool hall—just a few tables set up for eight-ball and rotation, wooden chairs and card tables scattered along the sides, and an ancient green canteen filled with bottles of soda. Beer was available at the counter. If you were hungry, you could purchase a dinner of fried chicken or smothered beefsteak, corn bread, and green salad for under a buck.

A. Z. was a tall, dark-skinned, handsomely built man. His customary attire was blue denim overalls and a white short-sleeved shirt. He spent the early hours of the evening glad-handing everyone who came in for a drink, dinner, or a round of pool, or just to pass the time. He laughed and joked with each patron for a few minutes before moving on. It wouldn't have taken a visitor long to see why A. Z. was the public relations point man for the Bogalusa movement.

Robert Hicks remembers installing A. Z. as president of the Bogalusa

Voters League after "eight or nine other people" had declined the position—presumably because of the great risks involved.* Bob himself did not want the presidency; he preferred to take the behind-the-scenes, coordinator role and let A. Z. stand before the cameras.

Some months before A. Z. passed away in 1993, at the age of seventy-three, the African American community in Bogalusa held an affair to honor him. Several of the speakers compared A. Z. favorably to Martin Luther King Jr. (who never made an appearance in Bogalusa). One woman, reflecting the general sentiment of the gathering, lauded A. Z. as the one true Bogalusa man of action. When the Bogalusa Voters League needed someone to lead a sit-in at a counter or a demonstration on Columbia Road, they looked to A. Z. The acclaim continued after his death. His body lay in state at the capitol rotunda in Baton Rouge. This was a tribute extended to no one else since Governor Earl K. Long in 1960. Later, the state welfare building in Baton Rouge was named after him.

A. Z. may have had neither the gift of reflection that Robert Hicks had nor the insight and inner strength of Gayle Jenkins. But to the crowd, A. Z. Young was the hero, the captain of the Bogalusa movement. A. Z. Young was in the spotlight while Bob and Gayle lingered in the media's shadows, and, although A. Z. is dead, the spotlight still shines on him today.

There are some people, and I include myself, who would question the assertion that A. Z. Young was the leader of the Bogalusa movement. To us A. Z. was a leader, certainly, but not *the* leader. He was not the only one who risked his life day after day: Robert Hicks and Gayle Jenkins were always out there with him. The night they honored A. Z., Robert Hicks did not attend; Gayle Jenkins did. Not one of the speakers said a word about Bob or Gayle.

After the Bogalusa movement ended, the governor invited A. Z. to

---

* Gayle Jenkins, in her interview with me on May 5, 1996, remembered that she asked A. Z. to become president after three or four other people had declined.

work for the state government in Baton Rouge. A.Z. accepted, and he eventually became director of the Division of Human Services for the Louisiana Health and Human Resources Administration. But throughout his career, "A.Z. never forgot his people," Gayle told me. A.Z. was there to the end—which in Gayle's opinion is the only way to live. "It's not the swift, but it's the one who endures to the end," she emphasized. In an apparent reference to other movement leaders, Gayle expressed disappointment: "I don't care all that he had done—if he put it down now, stopped, it don't count for nothing."

Every evening during that summer of 1966, men and women casually assembled around the tables and at the counter in Cozy Corners talking about the latest incidents: the boycotts, the injuries, the arrests, the Deacons' night patrols. I conversed with one group or another, including the CORE workers from California. But no matter what the conversations were about, I always had one ear tuned to the rhythms of Cannonball Adderley's "Mercy, Mercy, Mercy!" Bobby Moore's "Searching, Searching for My Baby," and Percy Sledge's "When a Man Loves a Woman" playing in succession on the radio. Late in the evening, after most people had gone home, A.Z. moved to a table in the corner of the room. Gayle and Bob joined him, and together they planned the next day's activities.

Among the four white CORE people who worked in Bogalusa were Tyrell Collins and Steve Wirtz. Both were college students from the San Francisco Bay Area. To me Tyrell Collins personified the hip Californian, the flower child of the sixties. I don't recall her ever wearing beads or a tie-dyed shirt, but she always dressed in bell-bottoms or jeans. Her large gold and black bangle earrings, highlighted against her dark blond hair, were her trademark.

Tyrell grew up in the San Fernando Valley of Los Angeles. Her mother, who raised Tyrell and her siblings as a single parent, had a strong belief in justice and fairness and imparted those values to her children. As a young woman, her mother had been a member of the

Communist Party—at a time when, as Tyrell said to me, the Russians were our allies and the party stood for social justice. Tyrell recalled the terror she felt when, as a little girl, she observed federal agents coming to her home and interviewing her mother, for reasons that she still could not fully explain.

When Tyrell was in high school, her brother was arrested in the Free Speech Movement in Berkeley. She saw on the six o'clock news her brother being dragged by his feet out of the administration building and down the steps. Although she was president of her senior class, Tyrell felt herself slipping away from the conventional. She had her ears pierced, bought a pair of wire-rimmed glasses, and switched from skirts to jeans. In college in Los Angeles she became politically active. In the summer of 1966, when she was nineteen, she moved to Berkeley to stay with her brother. She planned to attend school in San Francisco that fall.

In Berkeley, Tyrell saw a sign outside a church inviting people to a CORE-sponsored informational meeting on the movement in Louisiana. She volunteered. After an intense, challenging training session, she and three white male students were selected. They boarded a yellow school bus filled with clothes and food and rode it to Bogalusa. They donated the bus and its contents to the black community. Each of the student volunteers was assigned to live with a black family and to help with voter registration and the integration of public facilities.

Once Tyrell told me how a group of white toughs surrounded her and some black teenage girls after a demonstration in Bogalusa. One man asked her why she preferred niggers to whites. With fear in her heart, she replied that she was there to help, and that if he and his friends needed help, she would help them, too. Soon afterward they walked away.

At the time, given my idealism, I could not help but be intrigued by her conviction that love was the answer. I had read about flower power and love and peace imagery among the California hippies, but this was the first time I saw it in the flesh. Yet Tyrell did not fit into the languid

California hippie image; she was politically motivated, willing to come down to this alien Southern culture and try to change it. She had somehow been able to integrate the hippie philosophy of distancing herself from the previous generations' dishonest society with her own political philosophy of working for change within that society. We all had dreams back then, but somehow I believed Tyrell would fulfill hers.

Recently I met up with Tyrell again. She is married, with two sons, and is a painter living in the Bay Area. The day we met, she told me, she had seen a little orange kitten wandering in the neighborhood, a kitten that was too young to be straying outside. She stopped her car to retrieve it and then knocked on doors to locate the owner. At one house, the woman who answered the door exclaimed to her, "You think you can save the world. You can't save the world, you know." Tyrell responded ironically, "I can't ?" Thirty years after the end of the civil rights movement, our society has become infinitely more cynical. But there are people like Tyrell Collins who have never stopped believing they can make a difference. For Tyrell, love is still the answer.

Steve Wirtz also represented a stereotypical image to me—that of the committed student who believed that political action alone could make a difference. His was not a "flower power" approach. His beliefs in social justice were intense and earnest. Like Tyrell, Steve was a red-diaper baby. Steve's uncle, Willard Wirtz, whom Steve deeply admired, was secretary of labor in Lyndon Johnson's cabinet, but Steve's immediate family could not attend Willard's swearing-in ceremony. Texas senator John Tower had informed Willard that if Steve's father showed up, Tower would publicly reveal that Willard's brother had been a member of the Communist Party.*

I never met any young people in Louisiana who were members of the Communist Party. However, I did meet civil rights workers, like Tyrell and Steve, whose parents had been members. I also met several middle-aged people, many of them lawyers, who indicated that they had

* Today Steve Wirtz owns a prominent art gallery in San Francisco.

belonged to the Communist Party years before. They had joined the party because they saw it as the best hope for a more just and fair world, but most had become disillusioned over time and forsworn their memberships. Yet they were still troubled by the inequities of our nation's society, and the civil rights movement offered them the opportunity to pursue their quest for justice. I am fairly certain that some of the older people I met were still card-carrying members of the Communist Party. Now and then people would make casual references to belonging to the party, but no one revealed that information to me personally.

Listening to all the locals talk every evening at Cozy Corners about demonstrations, pickets, and boycotts intensified my desire to join in more exercises testing public accommodations. I did not have to wait long for an opportunity. Less than two weeks after the incident at the Acme Cafe, Charles Sims invited me to join him, his wife, and Tyrell in an attempt to integrate a beach along Lake Pontchartrain, near the town of Mandeville. I jumped at the chance. But that experience sobered me up very quickly: it compelled me to assess my place in the movement and to confront my choice of career. It taught me much more about the role of the lawyer and its inherent conflict with the role of the frontline activist. Even "activist lawyers," I learned, cannot really be both.

SIX

Stepping off
the Sidelines

Off we went! Charles Sims, the president of the Deacons for Defense and Justice; his wife, Bernice; Tyrell Collins; and me. As an integrated group, we were out to test the 1964 federal Civil Rights Act's prohibition against discrimination at a public beach on Lake Pontchartrain, near the town of Mandeville. It was July 31, 1966.

About fifteen miles outside Bogalusa, we spotted a whitewashed concrete block building and gas station. The sign out front read "Cold Beer." We stopped. The skinny, acne-faced white attendant stared at us, then turned away. We sat and waited. Three minutes passed. Charles Sims pressed on the horn. The boy looked up, then turned away again. Charles laid his hand on the horn a second time. The boy stayed by the doorway.

Charles Sims's contribution to the movement was not that of the typical civil rights leader. When I met him in 1966, his reputation as a loose cannon had preceded him. He was a man whose large stature was accompanied by a very short fuse. He had a rap sheet for mostly misdemeanor crimes and had been arrested for assault and carrying a concealed weapon. At various times he made his living by selling insurance. As a bachelor, he had described himself as a "party boy" with "plenty" of girls.[1] Although he was now married, he still flaunted his reputation as a ladies' man.

Because Sims was gruff, difficult, and unpredictable, people gave him a wide berth. When he took action, he did it with little, if any, reflection on the consequences. He had a commanding sense of entitlement. If his car needed gas, nothing would stop him from filling it up. If he wanted to sun himself on a beach, he would do it. Sims manifested his beliefs through action, not words. But his actions made a deafening roar.

I had several encounters with him, but there was one story that people always told about Sims—the one about his visit to New Orleans.

In 1965, when New Orleans restaurants were still heavily segregated, Charles Sims had come into town to purchase weapons for the Deacons. After completing their transactions, he and a colleague entered a well-known restaurant that was known not to serve blacks. Sims pulled a pistol out of his pocket and put it in the center of the table. He then called the waitress over. Within fifteen minutes, they were served. When they had finished eating, Sims and his friend lingered. The entire time, Sims kept that pistol resting on the table. After they had paid their bill and stood up from the table, Sims picked up the gun. No one crossed their path as they strolled out.

Now, at the gas station, Sims slowly squeezed out from the seat of his yellow, paint-chipped 1958 Chevy and walked up to the attendant. He motioned for the boy to follow him to the rear of the car. Bernice climbed out of the car and stood by the door. Not to be left out, Tyrell and I scrambled out too. When he reached the trunk, the boy close behind, Charles took out his key, turned the latch, and lifted the lid. I gasped.

Inside the trunk were a semiautomatic carbine that looked like a submachine gun, two shotguns, several boxes of shells, and a handful of grenades. No one said a word. The attendant backed away. Then he peered into the trunk again. I watched my life race before me. This was it, I thought. Sims would toss a grenade near the gas pump, and we would all go up in flames. Most assuredly Sims was capable of doing it. No one in Bogalusa would have been surprised.

The boy looked up at Sims. Sims glared back. The boy turned his eyes to the arsenal one more time and slowly walked to the gas cap. He unscrewed it, pulled down the nozzle from the gas pump, and filled up the tank. Only the rustling wind broke the silence. When the tank was full, he replaced the nozzle and closed the gas cap. And stayed put. Sims strode up to him and handed him a five-dollar bill. The attendant jogged over to the cash drawer, made change, and jogged back. Charles Sims took the change, stepped back to the trunk, slammed the lid shut, and climbed into the car. We followed. Sims started the engine, and off we drove.

In the car Tyrell and I started laughing, more as an expression of relief than of humor, recounting the scene. Sims, who had been silent until now, turned around in his seat and sternly warned us to calm down, admonishing us that life for African Americans in Louisiana was not a joke and that incidents like these do not always end so easily. "We could all have been killed," he swore. "And if some crackers care to follow us, we could still be."

My adrenaline was still racing when our car pulled into a parking lot by the beach at Lake Pontchartrain. We unloaded the car and walked onto the sand toward the water. When we found a comfortable spot, and one where others could easily observe us, we dug the beach umbrella into the sand. Then, after taking off our clothes to reveal our bathing suits, we set down a blanket and our towels. A white couple sitting nearby got up, collected their belongings, and moved a hundred yards down the beach. We chuckled. Bernice laid out a huge cloth and covered it with piles of fried chicken, cornbread, and strawberries. We were ready to picnic.

No sooner were we comfortable than a pink-faced sheriff in a brown uniform and black boots materialized at our side. I don't think any one of us had seen him coming. "You are all under arrest for changing on

the beach," he announced. As we looked up, still startled at his immediate though not unexpected presence, Tyrell protested. "We did not
change on the beach, we had our bathing suits on underneath our
clothes."

"Someone saw you change your clothes on the beach," he replied.

Tyrell spoke to me. "Peter, you're a lawyer, you take care of this."

I was not a lawyer. I was only a first-year law student, a big difference.
It was a crime to impersonate a lawyer, and I doubted that any local
judge would look kindly at my offense. There were no civil rights issues
involved in pretending to a police officer that I was an attorney. But I
played along.

"Who witnessed this event?" I asked. He would not tell me. I looked
around for possible "witnesses" and saw no one close by. Perhaps it was
that white couple who moved away, I thought. I asked him again. And
again he refused to reveal the name.

"As a lawyer, I have the right to know the name of the witness who
is bringing the charge," I reiterated. In fact, although it was true that
names of prosecution witnesses must be revealed, only the district attorney was required to provide them; police officers had no such obli-
gation. But, apparently young and green himself, out of his normal routine of arresting speeding motorists and drunken juveniles, the officer
appeared to be at a loss. Perhaps he also wondered whether he alone
could arrest us all without incident. He probably did not recognize
Charles Sims, but what if he had? Would it be a coup to arrest the
president of the Deacons, or would it be wiser to bow out of this scene
quickly? I couldn't help wondering what Charles would do if the officer
did try to arrest us. The arsenal in the trunk of the Chevy was out of
reach. But, knowing Charles's history, I figured he was packing a re-
volver in the pants that lay on the blanket. Would he reach for it?
Minutes passed as I badgered the officer for the witness's name. Charles
and the others remained silent.

Suddenly, without speaking another word, the officer turned and
walked away. He headed toward the parking lot, but I lost sight of him

as he passed behind some trees. We looked at each other, but nobody spoke. I feared he would return with reinforcements. Should we leave now before things got nasty?

But we could not leave. We still had a job to do, and unless we could demonstrate to the white community that we had taken a stand, that African Americans were entitled under civil rights laws to enjoy the beach as fully as white Americans, we wouldn't have finished our task. So we stayed put and ate our lunches. I could not concentrate on the food or the small talk. All I could think about was what would happen if the police officer learned that I was not an attorney: he would return and arrest me for impersonating an officer of the court.

Abruptly, after a hour had passed, Charles Sims said, "Let's go." He did not explain why he was ready to leave; that was not his nature. I assumed he felt we had established a clear presence at the beach, and he did not need to take photographs or otherwise document that we had done so. So, without many words spoken, we packed up our clothes, blankets, and beach umbrella. As we left, I thought I saw a state trooper's car parked at the other end of the road, but I could not be sure, and I did not care to mention it to anyone else.

We climbed into the Chevy with Sims behind the wheel and, keeping to the speed limit, drove back to Bogalusa. Trying not to be noticed, I kept glancing into the mirror to see whether anyone was following us. No one was. When we reached the outskirts of Bogalusa, Charles pressed his foot harder on the pedal, and within minutes we crossed Border Street. Whew!

Several days later, when I returned to New Orleans to file my Bogalusa reports, I told Richard Sobol, my supervisor at LCDC, about the incidents at the gas station and at the beach. He flew into a rage. He screamed at me that my job was to assist the black demonstrators and CORE civil rights workers when they were arrested and jailed, not to test integration cases. What good would it do if I were arrested and jailed along with them? I was needed to help release them from jail and then to collect evidence for the lawsuits against the local police and the

Ku Klux Klan. Richard assured me that if I ever were arrested, he would put me "on the next plane to New York."

I said nothing. He was my supervisor, and his rage intimidated me. When he had finished, I walked over to St. Charles Avenue and paced alongside the trolley tracks until I reached home. But Richard Sobol's reaction to my participation in these civil rights activities became a turning point in my life as a civil rights worker. I understood his logic; it was a lawyer's logic. Even after just one year of law school, I knew that it did not really matter what kind of law you participated in. All lawyers had to play by the rules. And the rules dictated that I stand on the sidelines taking notes. Listening to Richard reinforced my belief in action. I had watched people put their lives on the line, and I wanted to share some of the risks. Maybe I had skills they did not have. Maybe I would be more effective if I spent my time only on legal work. But I was learning a lot about myself that summer, about who I was and what was important to me. And I was learning that if lawyering meant standing apart, I would have to find something else to do with my life. In the meantime, I would straddle both worlds, marching in the lines sometimes and observing at other times, taking risks and taking notes.

I never let Richard or anyone else in the office know that I was continuing to participate in Bogalusa's demonstrations and testings. I took my chances that the movement people would not say anything to Richard and trusted that I could talk my way out of an arrest. Although I was not fully conscious of it then, I had already begun to distance myself from the practice of law. I had crossed a borderline, and I never really returned.

In April 1997 I discussed this episode with Lolis Elie—who, nearing seventy, still lives and practices law in New Orleans. He had invited me into his home several times to show me his marvelous collection of African art and sculpture, antislavery woodcuts, photographs of movement activists, and two magnificent portraits: one of Miles Davis, the other of Lolis himself, a regal man indeed. Lolis observed that "none of us lawyers were as progressive as you students," a fact that might explain the difference in attitudes between Richard Sobol and myself. True, we law students were generally more progressive in our thinking than practicing lawyers. But several of the lawyers, including Lolis, were more progressive than some of the students. And even the progressive students did not necessarily step off the sidelines and wade into the fray. Most of them never participated in integration testing or in demonstrations.

When I reminded Richard of this incident, he could not recall it. Obviously it was more important to me than to him. But he did assert that as chief staff counsel he definitely was not standing on the sidelines. Knowing that he represented clients in all kinds of civil rights situations, and that he once spent four hours in a Louisiana jail while representing a client, I can appreciate his perspective. But there are many kinds of activism, and Richard and I were defining it differently.

Looking back, I believe that the law students who stepped out of strictly legal roles and participated in civil rights activities helped forge a sense of confidence and trust between the civil rights legal organizations and the blacks in the community. We acted as liaisons and as ambassadors, and in doing so we bonded with the people we served. These days, when law firms reach out to the community, they call it client development. Client trust is essential to successful litigation. The supervising attorneys in the movement law offices, Richard included, needed to bond with the African American community if they were going to triumph. Richard Sobol was a lawyer's lawyer. The law students added that critical element of trust. In our extralegal roles and relationships, we built bridges across Border Street.

In retrospect I am thankful that Richard reacted as he did. His words helped me to consider more precisely my role in, and contribution to, the profession. I came to realize that it was not the practice of law itself that I was interested in. Rather, it was the opportunity to help others and to stand beside them.

SEVEN

Welcome to New Orleans

Twice during the summer of 1966 D'Army Bailey, the black Southern coordinator of the Law Students Civil Rights Research Council, came to New Orleans to meet with the law students. He wanted to stay apprised of our activities, to mediate any problems between law students and their supervisors, and to confirm that we were doing useful work. On this occasion, he called the LCDC office on Dryades Street and asked me to notify the other students that he was in town. We were to meet him the following evening for dinner at the Post House. None of us knew where it was.

Thirty years ago New Orleans did not have nearly the number or variety of restaurants it has today, but there were still plenty of first-rate places to eat. There were the oyster houses—such as Felix's (favored then), Acme (preferred today), and Messina's—where you were served platters of large, succulent Gulf oysters on the half-shell, shucked at the counter and served to order with lemon, ketchup, and horseradish. Then there were the deep-fried po'boy and muffaletta sandwich places such as Casamento's, the Napoleon House, and the Central Grocery Company. (A muffaletta included ham, mozzarella, pickles, marinated vegetables, relish, and olive oil on soft French bread.) Last, there were the upscale places we couldn't afford, like Brennan's for breakfast, Galatoire's, Antoine's, and Commander's Palace. We white civil rights workers didn't know many of the restaurants in the black neighborhoods other than those on Dryades Street, but the African American CORE workers in the office had not heard of the Post House either. We wondered why, with so many exceptional eateries around, D'Army had selected it. "Post House" certainly had no particular Creole or Cajun ring to it.

After checking the phone book, we discovered that Post House was the restaurant in the Greyhound bus terminal. We were aghast. Of all places to eat in New Orleans, the epicure's heaven, why there? Our first guess was that D'Army was a busy man and that he was only planning to stay long enough for dinner. Being efficient, he would board a bus immediately after dinner and move on. But then we heard he would be staying in town for several days.

Perhaps he did not know of another eatery, someone suggested, and this was as convenient as any other. But on reflection I suddenly understood his choice. The racist white Southern culture had had its effect even on this tough, assertive African American. He had chosen a white-owned restaurant that would serve African Americans without hesitation.

New Orleans restaurants had been nominally integrated in the early to mid-1960s as the result of several federal court decisions and the Civil Rights Act. However, people's comfort levels do not change by decree, and there was still a distinct, albeit unwritten, discrimination policy against blacks by white restaurateurs. Rarely, if ever, did mixed parties of blacks and whites enter a white establishment, even though such restaurants often employed black cooks and black waiters (but never black cashiers). The blacks had their place, and it was not sitting at the tables. When mixed parties of blacks and whites wanted to eat out together, they went to black establishments in black neighborhoods.

The Post House, where we met D'Army Bailey, had the weight and force of federal law behind it. As a restaurant linked physically and economically to an interstate bus depot, it was a part of interstate commerce. It was therefore directly and obviously subject to the Civil Rights Act of 1964. Of course, the federal civil rights law had been interpreted to apply to nearly every major restaurant in the country, including those of New Orleans. Nevertheless, the Post House would be more likely to serve African Americans willingly than would other restaurants in New Orleans that relied on the local white population for their goodwill and economic survival. D'Army could be comfortable there, and we would be much less likely to have a belligerent encounter with white customers or staff.

There was also perhaps another reason why D'Army did not choose a black establishment for dinner: to emphasize again the effects of Southern white culture on African Americans. In deciding on the Post House, D'Army was essentially reminding us of what he had said during orientation in Mississippi. When the summer was over, we would no longer have to confront or even think about what it means to be excluded from mainstream culture day after day. In the South, blacks would still be constantly reminded of their place in the racist culture.

Around ten o'clock that evening, four of us law students walked back from dinner to the apartment we shared on Bourbon Street. Suddenly we heard groans from down the street, a block from Jackson Park. We ran over. Two white members of New Orleans's finest were pushing and pummeling a black man against the wall of a building. We stood there, our mouths hanging open, watching intently but saying nothing. Within sixty seconds, one of the cops noticed us. "Hey, what are you looking at?" he called out. One of us blurted out, "We're just observing the arrest. We're law students."

Those were not the wisest words we could have chosen. The cop glared at us and barked, "Get the hell out of here now or we'll arrest all of you too." And his tone made it very clear that "arrest" meant more than a lockup. It did not take much to convince us that it was time to leave. We sprinted down the street. When we turned the corner onto Bourbon Street, one of us suggested filing a report with the New Orleans police department and with the LSCRRC. We all concurred. But we never did.

Why didn't we file the report? I don't know about the other students, but I didn't trust the police to respond fairly to a charge of brutality. I was terrified that instead they would retaliate by coming to look for us. I'm smiling as I write this. There I was, the grand activist standing up and taking risks with the blacks in Bogalusa, and then running away on the streets of New Orleans. I can't say that my behavior was consistent. I guess I crossed borderlines some days and crossed back on other days.

The apartment the four of us were headed home to was on lower Bourbon Street, a few blocks from Esplanade Avenue, at the edge of the French Quarter. One of my roommates, David Strand, had the enviable assignment of working on civil rights and civil liberties cases for Ben Smith.

Ben Smith was a renowned white lawyer for the movement. In 1963 he had been arrested and charged under Louisiana's Communist Control Act with failing to register as a member of two "Communist front organizations" and for acting as treasurer of a "subversive organization." One organization was the Southern Conference Educational Fund (SCEA). According to the police, the SCEA was essentially the same as the Southern Conference for Human Welfare (SCHW), which had been cited by committees of the United States Congress as a Communist front organization. In fact, the SCHW was an interracial group of Southerners who, beginning in the late 1930s and early 1940s, campaigned to end segregation. The members of SCHW created SCEA in 1946 to promote educational approaches toward this goal.[1] The other organization was the National Lawyers Guild, a group of progressive attorneys. The guild had been designated by committees of the United States Congress as a Communist front organization, but that designation was rescinded by the United States attorney general in 1958.[2]

The police raid in which Smith was arrested occurred on the same day as a National Lawyers Guild workshop on civil rights cases just outside New Orleans. Police officers and trusties (convicts) from the New Orleans House of Detention, acting under the direct supervision of the staff director and the counsel for the state Un-American Activities Committee, ransacked Smith's home and office at gunpoint, along with the homes and offices of two other members of the Southern Conference Educational Fund: James Dombrowski, the fund's executive director, and Bruce Waltzer, Smith's law partner. Leander Perez Sr. (the segregationist who later persuaded officials in Plaquemines Parish to jail Richard Sobol for the unlicensed practice of law) was also understood to be behind the raid. Among the items confiscated were subscription lists, SCEA membership lists, records, a copy of Thoreau's journal, a Hebrew Bible, Greek books, and a copy of the Declaration of Independence signed by Franklin Roosevelt. The chairman of the Un-American Activities Committee announced that the raids and arrest resulted from "racial agitation."

Dombrowski, Waltzer, and Smith filed suit in federal court to enjoin the prosecutions. *Dombrowski v Pfister* went to the Supreme Court in 1965. The Court decided in their favor, recognizing that the state's prosecution had a "chilling effect" on their exercise of their First Amendment rights of free speech and association. In finding the state's Communist Control Act void, the Court restrained the state authorities from prosecuting the plaintiffs.[3] The Court understood that to allow the state to harass Ben Smith and the others under the ill-defined Communist Control Act would effectively suppress representation for civil rights workers: few lawyers would be willing to defend such cases if they risked prosecution.

Born in the northern Louisiana town of Ruston, Ben Smith passionately defended the civil rights and liberties of all people, black or white. I knew no one who could say he had ever compromised his integrity. Although his foes may have been hostile—sometimes even the judges were contemptuous of him and what he stood for—Ben Smith treated everyone with charm and grace. In 1965 he was an attorney for the Mississippi Freedom Democratic Party, which fought to include blacks in the voting process. When I arrived in New Orleans in the summer of 1966, he was already a local legend. We were honored whenever he and his wife, Corinne, invited us to their Garden District home to discuss a civil rights case in which Ben and LCDC were involved. He later became president of the Center for Constitutional Rights in New York. Ben Smith died in 1976 at the age of forty-eight.

David Strand told us while he was working for Ben that his goal was to become mayor of Cleveland. I don't know whether David ever became mayor; his cheerful personality would have given him a decided edge over other candidates. Another of my roommates on Bourbon Street was Frank Dubofsky, a student at Georgetown Law School. He only stayed for three weeks while waiting for the Law Student Civil Rights Research Council to confirm his placement with Murphy Bell, a black attorney in Baton Rouge. Frank was great company during that short time; he was forever regaling us with stories. One of my favorites was how he had failed to become an all-American football hero at Stanford.

Frank had nearly made the all-American team as a junior, and the media had targeted him in the beginning of his senior year as a preseason all-American. In fall 1963, at the start of Frank's senior year, the football coach gave the team a vigorous pep talk before the first game. The coach railed on and on that Saturday's contest would be the most important event of their lives. Yet the more Frank heard, the more he lost heart.

Although it was still early in the sixties, it was clear to Frank that the world was changing dramatically. For days during the Cuban missile crisis we had anticipated annihilation by nuclear holocaust. Sit-ins at lunch counters had sparked national awareness of the cruelties of segregation; interracial groups of "Freedom Riders" had risked their lives by riding buses into the Southern states; Martin Luther King and his followers had been attacked with police dogs and fire hoses, the brutality spotlighted on national television. And Frank was being told that this football game was the most important milestone in his life. As the coach droned on, Frank rose, collected his gear, walked out of the locker room, and never returned.

To get to our apartment, we had to pass through a carved oak door with a frosted leaded-glass window. Above the door rose a seashell-shaped arch, enclosing another leaded-glass window, this one clear. Louvered shutters covered the four windows facing the street. The door led into a courtyard fragrant with red-flowered banana trees, red and white hibiscus, and purple bougainvilleas. Many of the houses in the French Quarter were hidden gems. But to us urban renters, the greatest pleasure in that courtyard was the oval-shaped swimming pool, ringed by pretty copper-colored flagstones.

Bourbon Street was, and is, the best-known street in the sixty-four blocks of the Vieux Carré, the French Quarter. On Bourbon Street cadaverous barkers stood outside the "topless and bottomless" clubs each night, their grubby fingers holding the red curtains open just far enough for you to peek in and catch a glimpse of flesh. From seven in the evening until two in the morning, the barkers beckoned you inside to have a drink and be "entertained" while the clubs blasted the "dance and performance" music into the street.

On Bourbon Street drunken tourists sang on the sidewalks and in the street, while drunken locals sang and partied on the balconies above. It was de rigueur to carry a drink while meandering along the street. Tourists carried the obligatory hurricane glass filled with four ounces of rum and passion fruit, or mint julep, or both—one in each hand—from Pat O'Brien's around the corner. (Today, in some drinking spots, the old hurricane glass has yielded to the paper cup for street parties.)

But Bourbon Street was more than raunchy. It was also the street where trumpeter Al Hirt and clarinetist Pete Fountain held court nightly. Any time after ten o'clock, these masters would blow their horns, the sounds wafting through the clubs' open doorways and into the night air, seducing passersby. And on the corner of Bourbon and

Toulouse stood the 544 Club where Clarence "Frogman" Henry, who earned his fifteen minutes of fame with his top-ten hits "Don't Know Why I Love You But I Do" and "Ain't Got No Home," sang his heart out every night.

Thirty steps around the corner of Bourbon Street and down St. Peter Street stood Preservation Hall, the dilapidated building that embodied the spirit of New Orleans. Its windows were laden with dirt and dust. Iron strap hinges secured the shutters and doors. But every evening, these creaky, aged shutters and doors burst open to glorious syncopated jazz rhythms. Starting at about seven-thirty, when most of the locals had not even begun contemplating what to make for dinner, tourists would begin to queue outside the building. As the night grew dark, the queue snaked down the block and onto Royal Street.

To enter the hall, we passed through a wrought-iron gate leading into an alley, one wall of which was lined with old gas meters and exposed gas lines. This was the only entrance and exit. Usually two people, a man and a woman, were standing inside the gate holding straw baskets. We dropped in a dollar bill and pressed closer to the music.

Although New Orleans was looked on as more open and cosmopolitan than other Southern cities, there was still only a handful of local residents to whom civil rights people could reach out. I got to know most of them, and I soon realized that the people collecting the money at Preservation Hall were allied with the civil rights movement; the money the club earned would go not only to the musicians but also to civil rights causes.

At an intermission, usually every half-hour, people pushed their way from the alley through one of two heavy oak doorways leading to the front or the back of the hall. Standing outside the building or in the alleyway—sometimes for hours—was worth it. We didn't have to see the musicians to feel the music, the divine toe-tapping, head-bobbing, and syncopated rhythms. We were there.

Inside the crowded, nearly windowless room, perhaps the size of a high school classroom, the old men played their trumpets, clarinets, trombones, pianos, and bass fiddles, transporting us back to a bygone era, the 1920s and 1930s. Many of the musicians were seventy or eighty, even ninety years old, but they still played hotter music than anyone else in the Quarter. I visited Preservation Hall as often as I could. I never tired of the music, the stories, and the ambience. And it seemed safe: a place blacks and whites could go together and not feel threatened.

Still, New Orleans's pretense of interracial harmony was only that—a veneer. Blacks were still expected to stay in their own neighborhoods. So when integrated groups stepped into white establishments, they were asking for trouble. This was especially true when they went drinking in local bars.

One night, several of us law students accompanied an interracial American Friends Service Committee group to a local Decatur Street bar, across from the old Jax Brewery. Decatur Street was one of the scruffier streets in the Quarter; it ran along the Mississippi River. Two people belonging to the Friends group were African American. We sat down. Five or ten minutes passed, but no waiter stopped by. After fifteen minutes it became abundantly clear that the white waiter was not going to serve us. We watched as he gossiped, perhaps about us, with the other patrons. This was a typical working-class bar—a bad choice for visiting with mixed racial company. Finally, one of the law students, whom I'll call Paul, a person with an incredibly short fuse, spoke up so that everyone in the bar could hear him. "Hey, waiter," he called. When the waiter refused to come, Paul promptly labeled him a "racist."

People outside the movement sometimes revered civil rights workers. But we were simply human beings with human strengths and human failings. Of course there were individuals like Martin Luther King, whose love and self-discipline were exceptional. But the movement was not doctrinaire by nature. All its members had in common were our beliefs and actions in the cause. Thus it had its good-hearted people who in the stress of the moment sometimes acted unthinkingly. Paul was one such person.

The waiter responded by drawing his sweaty body close to Paul, asking, "What did you say?" Weighing over two hundred pounds and standing over six feet tall, Paul had no compunctions about repeating himself. "I said you're a racist." Without a word, the waiter threw a punch at Paul's head. Then he turned and walked away. Paul picked up a bottle of beer and hurled it at the waiter. It missed, but that didn't matter. Several of the burly patrons descended on Paul. As he pushed his way free, we all jumped up, headed for the door, and tore down the street. The waiter and his drinking buddies hollered in pursuit. We raced around one corner and turned another. Our pursuers must have been too drunk and too out of shape to keep up with us, because we got away. Paul wanted us to return the next evening with baseball bats, but no one would join him.

Welcome to New Orleans, I thought that night. Its music and food were exhilarating. But scratch its surface and you'd find the same territorial racism prevalent in any other Southern town. New Orleans did not need a Border Street to divide the black and white communities.

EIGHT

Litigating the End to Segregation

No matter how early my day began, it was always hot and muggy when I went to work at the LCDC office. I always loved the mornings in New Orleans, the French Quarter grit, the tropical weather, the greasy breakfasts that somehow invigorated and prepared me for the day to come. I would leave my apartment on Bourbon Street and wander up toward Canal Street. From there, if I felt in a New York mood, I'd head up Bourbon and stop at a little hole-in-the-wall counter shop with four stools. There, echoing my breakfast habits from the streets of New York, I'd purchase orange juice served in a paper cup that sat in a cone-shaped plastic gray container, chocolate milk served in the same kind of cup, and a chocolate glazed donut. I'd lean against the narrow counter, savor the sugar and grease, and watch the local shopkeepers sweep up last night's detritus of candy wrappers, broken hurricane glasses, dried vomit, and used condoms before hosing down the sidewalks.

Then the garbage trucks would clank by on the narrow cobblestone streets, stopping every fifty or so feet to uncork a star-and-crescent-detailed manhole cover (because the Mississippi River snakes around the city in the shape of a crescent, New Orleans is called the "Crescent City") and lift out the sunken garbage can. Positioning the cans under the sidewalk kept them safe from drunken revelers who would inevitably have knocked them over. It also helped keep vermin at bay, but it meant that passersby had to lift the heavy manhole covers to deposit their litter.

If I was in a New Orleans mood, I would take a detour off Bourbon Street, down St. Ann Street, and, strolling over a cobblestone walkway and under some of the loveliest wrought-iron balconies in the French Quarter, head toward the Café Du Monde by the Mississippi River on Decatur Street. Horses and carriages lined up across the street, in front of Jackson Square, awaiting the day's tourists. Local artists collected along the edges of the park offering to draw quick sketches of tourists. The old Jax Brewery—which has since taken its cue from other "inspired" downtown improvements and become a mini-mall—faced the cafe from just up the street. And here, at the tiny take-out window, I would begin my day with an order of three beignets. Even when I had the time to sit in the outdoor cafe, I always ordered at the take-out window. I was used to eating breakfast on the run in New York, and I could not imagine doing otherwise in New Orleans. The cafe also served its unique blend of chicory and coffee, but, alas, I was a chocoholic and ordered that container of chocolate milk every time.

Those hot, humid, gritty mornings were surreal, sensual, and brilliant with color. Refreshed, I would proceed on my walk through the Quarter, passing the phone booths where, thanks to Huey Long and his populist legacy, local calls were still only a nickel. Each time the local phone company tried to raise the cost to a dime, to match the cost everywhere else in the country, the Louisiana Public Utilities Commission denied the application. We loved it, and so did the locals, who kept reelecting the same members of the commission. But the phone company had the last laugh with long-distance calls. The cost of those calls made up the difference, and then some.

When I reached Canal Street—the widest street in the United States, I was told back then—I again had a choice. If I was running late, I would catch the bus that took me within half a block of the LCDC office on

Dryades Street. If I needed to absorb more New Orleans charm before I was ready to settle down to work, I'd catch one of the picture-postcard olive green cars of the St. Charles trolley.

From my old-fashioned yet very comfortable wooden seat on the trolley, I would peer out at the once-elegant antebellum mansions lining St. Charles Avenue and the ancient live oak trees that enveloped them. Now and then I would spot a banana tree or some yellow hibiscus peeking from the backyards.

The St. Charles trolley skirted the edges of the Garden District, where at one time the New Orleans gentry made their homes. Even today many of the city's elite reside here. I would disembark at Jackson Avenue and walk the few blocks to Dryades. But if the day was just too grand and nothing was pressing at the office, I'd turn in the other direction and spend a few minutes exploring the neighborhood.

One time I turned a corner and walked up to the Lafayette Cemetery, its soot-blackened red brick and peeling stucco mausoleums and tombs all erected above the swampy ground below. Since New Orleans lies below sea level, it has had to build its burying places above ground—or find bodies floating in the local waters. For the poor, simple, artless vaults were built to stack the bodies like cordwood, perhaps eight or ten high. Even the richly designed tombs constructed for the city's elite families held many more bodies than the names inscribed on the stone, for when epidemics raced through the city no one had time for formal burials. If you looked carefully, you could find a button or a shard of bone from a decayed corpse that had floated up into the dirt.*

I'd walk the crumbling sidewalks, looking down rather than up for the names of the streets in the Garden District, hoping that I would find the name laid out in blue lettering on white tile. I was charmed by

---

* At one time, oak caskets were buried in the ground. But because the water level was often within three feet of the topsoil, the coffins decayed, exposing the bodies. When families used the same tomb for several generations of family members, they often removed the bones of a decomposed body, placed the bones in a bag, and buried the bag. The bags, too, eventually disintegrated, exposing the bones.

the names themselves. A year later, a local friend explained how the person who planned the lower Garden District grid in the 1800s named nine streets after the Greek muses: Calliope, Clio, Erato, Euterpe, Melpomene, Polymnia (for Polyhymnia), Terpsichore, Thalia, and Urania. Elegance and grit. Soulful music, food, and funk. Perhaps that was why I fell in love with New Orleans the day I arrived.

My work at LCDC was never the same from day to day. Sometimes I was drafting a memorandum or court brief. At other times Richard Sobol might tell me to drop everything else and draft affidavits supporting Bogalusa civil rights workers who had been injured in one melee or another. Besides litigating against the Bogalusa and Washington Parish police departments and the Ku Klux Klan, LCDC sued to integrate the schools in Bogalusa and other Louisiana communities, to integrate the workforce at the Crown Zellerbach mill in Bogalusa, and to integrate public accommodations and facilities. And, of course, Sobol and his staff were always there to defend civil rights workers who had been unjustly arrested and to handle the demonstrators' appeals if they were convicted by the local courts.

Although the *Brown v Board of Education* decision against "separate but equal" facilities was twelve years old in 1966, only a handful of black children had been integrated into the Southern white school systems. The federal Department of Health, Education, and Welfare (HEW) had instituted guidelines for integrating the schools, but integration was met with massive resistance from nearly every school district.

Until 1966, the common procedure to integrate the Southern schools was for a black family to apply for their children's transfer to a white school. But because of harassment and intimidation, hardly any black parents in the South had done so. In Bogalusa, for example, only three black students attended Bogalusa High School, and only two black students broke the color barrier at the local elementary school in 1965.[1]

In 1966, the federal courts adopted HEW's guidelines and required school districts to offer a "freedom-of-choice" plan. Parents were entitled to select the school their children should attend. The choice was essentially between a formerly all-white school or a formerly all-black school. Although the white schools had received significantly more funding over the years, had facilities far superior to those of black schools, and were universally considered to provide a better education, very few African American parents selected them. White resistance included threats as well as actual incidents of violence and intimidation. In addition, black parents feared losing their jobs if they sent their children to all-white schools. African American parents who did send their children to white schools were seen by the courts as people with "exceptional initiative and fortitude."[2]

The local school districts made it administratively burdensome for African American parents to receive the freedom-of-choice forms and to fill them out "correctly." District offices often required that the forms be notarized and that the parents submit official birth and health certificates. Even where parents did succeed in sending their children to the white schools, the children were often exiled to separate sections of the classrooms and schoolyards, making their day-to-day experiences miserable. Because the freedom-of-choice plan encountered heavy resistance, HEW was unable to persuade school boards to take more forceful action to integrate the schools.

Richard Sobol chose Rick Seymour, a law student from Harvard and another summer roommate of mine, to work on LCDC's school desegregation cases. Much of Rick's time was spent writing motions to force the state of Louisiana to equalize spending for black and white school districts. Richard and Rick hoped that by making it more expensive to maintain separate school systems, they could pressure the state into integrating them. Rick impressed Richard and other people in the office by figuring out that LCDC could significantly increase the number of court filings in school discrimination cases by merely whiting out the names of one set of parties on the court papers, photocopying them, and then writing in the names of another set of parties from another parish. Thus LCDC was able to create and file legal documents in seventeen school desegregation cases in less than a month—an impressive feat in the days before word-processing. When Rick was not working in the office, he drove up to northern Louisiana with either Richard Haley, CORE's Southern director, or Ike Reynolds, CORE's field secretary. They would try to convince African Americans there to become plaintiffs in LCDC lawsuits against their school districts.

Perhaps part of the reason for Rick Seymour's dedication to the workings of the law was his belief in the Republican Party, a somewhat foreign concept to most of us in the movement. Rick was from Grand Rapids, Michigan, "the furniture capital of the world," as he put it; he was a political eccentric among civil rights workers. He never hesitated to remind us that it was Lincoln's Republicans who freed the slaves and that it was the Republicans who believed in the strength of the individual. And ultimately, he thought, black culture would benefit more from the Republican philosophy promoting the strong, self-motivated individual than from the Democratic Party's well-meaning but paternalistic attitude. To people who see many of today's racial problems as descending from the actions of sixties liberals who had good intentions but poor planning, failed vision, and a limited understanding of human nature, Rick Seymour appears to have been right.*

On August 16, 1966, the federal district court judge Frederick J. R. Heebe ordered a freedom-of-choice plan in Bogalusa. He also required that the bus routes serve all pupils and that remedial educational programs be established to help black students catch up to the superior white education. However, as in other Southern communities, his order made little difference. Only eighty-five black students entered the white schools that fall, fifty of whom entered the local junior high. There were tense confrontations between armed black and white parents outside the junior high school that September. At one point a white man pointed a

* Today Rick Seymour is the director of the Employment Discrimination Project for the Lawyers' Committee in Washington, D.C. He has litigated a large number of high-impact employment discrimination cases, including many that have been decided by the U.S. Supreme Court.

rifle at Royan Burris, the vice president of the Deacons. That prompted the blacks to rush to the trunk of a car and haul out rifles. Several whites then drew pistols from their pockets. Fortunately, the local police dispersed the groups before anyone got hurt.[3]

Racial incidents occurred within the school as well. Five black boys who wanted to try out for the football team had become too afraid to attend practice. When one of the boys told A. Z. Young, "They're not gonna let us play nohow," A. Z. counseled them, "You got to stay with it. If you back up now we gotta go through all this again next year."[4]

There was even greater resistance to integration of the faculties at the schools, particularly to the hiring of African American teachers at the white schools. The school board president felt that it was too inflammatory an issue to deal with at the moment: integrating the students was as far as they could go. Thus in the fall of 1966 no black teacher was hired to teach in the white schools of Bogalusa.

Progress in integrating the schools was finally made in December 1966, when the United States Court of Appeals for the Fifth Circuit—an activist court that heard nearly all the appeals of the vital civil rights cases of the decade—ruled that integration of the Southern school systems was moving too slowly. To speed up the process, the court decreed significant changes in school integration. The case was *United States v Jefferson County Board of Education*,[5] and, as in the Bogalusa *Ku Klux Klan* injunction case, the respected judge John Minor Wisdom took the lead in advancing the rights of blacks. Early in his opinion Judge Wisdom recognized that "no court can have a confident solution for a legal problem so closely interwoven with political, social and moral threads as the problem of establishing fair, workable standards for undoing de jure school segregation in the South."[6] Nevertheless, Judge Wisdom felt that the court had to act and that school boards had affirmative duties to make the changes needed to integrate the schools. White schools and black schools were to be abolished and replaced by "unitary nonracial" single school systems.

Although Wisdom still allowed for freedom-of-choice plans, he also recommended that school boards take the initiative to institute other programs, such as the pairing of schools. The federal appeals court also required school districts to integrate faculties, encouraging white teachers to teach in mixed schools, and to integrate the facilities and activities, including athletics and interscholastic associations. In effect, Wisdom said that school districts needed to take decisive action using tough new standards to integrate the schools. They could no longer passively wait for the parents to act. "The only school desegregation plan that meets constitutional standards is one that works," wrote Judge Wisdom.[7] Beginning in 1967, LCDC, under Richard Sobol, drew on Judge Wisdom's opinion in formulating strategies for integrating the Bogalusa school system as well as for researching possible litigation in other Louisiana communities.

LCDC also pursued employment discrimination cases, and one of the biggest of the late 1960s was the Crown Zellerbach case. Of the 2,760 employees at the Crown mill in Bogalusa, 400 were African American. Until 1966, the mill had separate "lines of progression" for white and black workers. No matter how long a black worker was employed at the mill, he would never be promoted above a white worker with less seniority.* And the better-paying and more desirable jobs were reserved for whites. One of the plaintiffs in the case had been employed at the mill for over twenty-seven years, yet his highest position was as a "temporary" helper. The local unions representing the workers were also racially segregated. The plant maintained segregated shower, locker, and lavatory facilities, providing superior facilities for whites.

In 1966, Crown nominally merged the black and white lines of progression. But since blacks had been given undesirable, lower-paying, unskilled jobs before the lines were merged, they still lagged behind whites in advancement. In addition, Crown created new barriers to equal

---

* According to Bob Hicks, except for one woman who worked as a maid cleaning the company guesthouse, no black women worked for the mill until years later, when the lawsuits against Crown were settled (phone conversation, August 11, 1999).

employment. It adopted personnel tests as a condition of employment and advancement and created "trainee" groups in each department, admission to which was limited to white employees. After completing "trainee" sessions, the white employees could leapfrog past black employees with greater seniority.

In June 1966, Robert Hicks became the lead plaintiff in an action against Crown Zellerbach, the International Brotherhood of Pulp, Sulphite and Paper Mill Workers, the AFL-CIO, and the Magic City Local union. A. Z. Young and several other workers joined in the lawsuit a year later. Between 1966 and 1970, Richard Sobol and LCDC litigated against a barricade of procedural and substantive issues raised by the attorneys for Crown to forestall the integration of the Bogalusa plant's workforce. Although its principal offices were in San Francisco, one of the most enlightened cities in the country, Crown fought every inch of the way. Richard Sobol filed much of the litigation. But it was only in 1971, two years after Sobol left LCDC, that Judge Heebe issued his major, comprehensive decision on the merits of the case in favor of the black employees.

Judge Heebe relied on Title VII of the Civil Rights Act of 1964, which outlawed discrimination in employment. The act read that it was an unlawful employment practice for an employer "to limit, segregate, or classify his employees in any way which would tend to deprive any individual of employment opportunities . . . because of his race." He proscribed the battery of tests that Crown had instituted as a condition of employment and promotion. He noted that blacks who wanted to transfer to jobs from which they had been previously excluded under the old segregated system had to take these tests, whereas whites who had been in the white line of progression prior to the integration of the two lines did not. Heebe also held that although the content of the tests was not shown to be racially biased, the effect of the tests was to exclude all but a small number of blacks. Crown had shown no justification or "business necessity" for the tests. Thus, in order for Crown to use such tests, it had to show that the skills they measured were relevant to

Crown's job performance needs. Crown was ordered to undertake a careful professional study of the validity and reasonableness of the tests. The company did not.

As Judge Heebe wrote, "This discrimination between contemporaneously hired whites and Negroes is the baldest form of discrimination. Defendants forced Negro workers into less desirable jobs. When this official segregation was lifted, the company imposed a new testing requirement on present employees wishing to transfer—a requirement having its primary, if not total, impact on formerly segregated Negroes wishing to improve their job status."

Heebe also ruled that Crown could not require black employees to take a reduction in pay when they were transferred to an entry-level job in the formerly white-only lines of progression. He also reaffirmed his earlier preliminary and permanent injunctions merging the two local black and white unions, replacing job seniority with "total plant seniority," and enjoining the battery of tests given to black workers until they were validated in accordance with Equal Employment Opportunity Commission (EEOC) guidelines.

Although the mill was entirely segregated, and although the black workers had the lowest-paying and the least desirable jobs at the mill, I nevertheless believed, disheartening as it might sound, that the mill was a relative boon to the local black community. Because so many black men were employed there and took home regular paychecks, including Robert Hicks, A. Z. Young, and Monroe Jenkins (Gayle's husband), the mill allowed the African Americans in Bogalusa to take risks that African Americans in other Southern communities could not. The company may have erected legal obstructions all through litigation, but its headquarters were still far enough away from the action to escape direct influence by the local white racist culture. Thus, it was not as likely that an African American employee who stood up to the white man would be fired from his job as it would have been in other communities where unskilled black laborers were dependent on the whims of local white employers. Crown Zellerbach needed these men to do the "dirty" work that whites refused to do. That relative economic security allowed blacks in Bogalusa to participate with more confidence in the boycotts of the local white-owned shops on Columbia Road, to register to vote, to send their children to the formerly all-white schools, and even to join or at least support the Deacons for Defense in their armed guard against the Klan.

Beyond the day-to-day litigation strategies, the civil rights movement offered true intellectual challenges, and Richard Sobol thrived on them. Often he would be in contact with Charles Nesson at Harvard and Anthony (Tony) Amsterdam, then at the University of Pennsylvania and now at New York University School of Law. From their ivory towers these two "guru" professors guided the movement's litigation. They offered suggestions on how to defeat local segregationist laws and assembled arguments for appeals to the higher courts.

Tony Amsterdam could reel off United States Supreme Court citations like the days of the week. He seemed to have instant recall of every Supreme Court decision and its relevance to the legal issue before us. Tony spun his legal web back in Philadelphia, and, spreading it over the state, we caught many a racist fly in Louisiana.

One of the most valuable tactics that civil rights lawyers had used during the early days of the movement, and a tactic that Richard Sobol, Charles Nesson, and Tony Amsterdam spent countless hours discussing, was "removing" state cases; that is, transferring state cases to federal court. Under a post–Civil War federal law,[8] defendants who claimed that they could not obtain a fair trial in state court, because of discriminatory state policy or discriminatory action by state officials in advance of trial, could have the case transferred to federal court. Because federal judges held their positions for life, they were less susceptible to local pressures and prejudices than state judges. Hence in the federal court the defendant could expect a fairer and more professional hearing.

Civil rights lawyers employed this federal statute as much as they could. Removal was automatic: all the civil rights attorney had to do was file the appropriate papers. The burden would then shift to the state to argue that the case should not have been removed. In arguing that cases should remain in federal court, the civil rights attorneys insisted that any defendant who was arrested in a civil rights matter could not possibly obtain a fair trial in a state court proceeding, since the state, as well as the local cities and towns, fostered a continual policy of racial discrimination against blacks and civil rights workers through its laws and its implementation of these laws. The civil rights lawyers pointed out that black defendants and white civil rights workers were often arrested on trumped-up charges such as "disturbing the peace," "trespass," or "vagrancy" solely for the purpose of harassment.

The federal removal statute offered significant tactical advantages. First, many of those arrested were held on exorbitant bail; "removal" freed civil rights workers without requiring any bond money or security. They could then swiftly return to their work in the movement. Second, even when the state's attorney succeeded in remanding the case back to state court, so much time had elapsed that the prosecution had often lost its edge in securing witnesses and other evidence. The prosecutor was therefore more likely to drop the charges or agree to a plea bargain on a reduced charge and minimal punishment.

Unfortunately, on June 20, 1966, when I had been in the South for about a month, the U.S. Supreme Court, in *City of Greenwood, Mississippi v Peacock* limited the circumstances in which we could remove cases to federal court.[9] But that did not stop Richard Sobol. He immediately began figuring out how to circumvent the *Peacock* decision. The legal complexities raised by the case continued to intrigue him. In July 1968 his work paid off. Richard Sobol persuaded the U.S. Court of Appeals for the Fifth Circuit to allow the removal of state criminal proceedings to federal court whenever civil rights workers could establish that they were being prosecuted by the state as a way to punish them for encouraging people to register and vote.[10]

NINE

Hiroshima Vigil

During the summer, I and my roommate David Bresnick, a third-year law student at Columbia University who worked in the LCDC office, joined up with students from Tulane University who sympathized with the movement. Besides civil rights, we talked about the Vietnam War and American politics. It didn't take long for someone to suggest that we commemorate the anniversary of the atomic bombing of Hiroshima on August 6, 1945, and protest the rapidly escalating war in Vietnam. So about twenty of us, including Tyrell Collins, who took a bus down from Bogalusa, decided to hold a twenty-four-hour vigil.

Protesting against the war was a seamless extension of my civil rights stance. On a practical level, it was apparent by 1966 that the nation was squandering resources on a conflict eight thousand miles away, resources that could have been used in the civil rights movement and in President Johnson's war on poverty. On a more cynical level, we had to question why our government was burning, bombing, and napalming people in village huts in a tiny country in Southeast Asia and supporting Saigon's puppet dictators in the name of "peace and democracy" while focusing less and less attention on the critical issue of racial injustice at home.

On the night of August 5, we lined up in front of the Molly Marine statue at Canal Street and Elks Place. Several of us held signs that recounted the number of people killed and maimed in Hiroshima, while others held peace signs with drawings of doves. We all gave the "V" sign to passersby.

The vigil, which began at midnight, received limited media attention. Occasionally local thugs drove by and verbally harassed us, calling us "Commies" and "faggots." Otherwise things went along quietly until mid-morning on August 6. At 10 A.M. a short, slightly built man drove up. He was maybe thirty years old, in a red and white striped shirt and blue trousers. He stepped out of his car carrying a camera, made a few notes on a pad, and walked up to the first person in the line. From about two feet away the cameraman snapped a head shot. He then walked up to the second person and snapped his photo. We stood there stunned, not understanding what was going on. He continued down the line, photographing everyone.

Since we had pledged to maintain twenty-four hours of silence, no one challenged him. Finally, because I was a law student and a paranoid one at that, I left the line and asked him what he was doing and whether he was a reporter or worked for the New Orleans Police Department or the FBI. He ignored all my questions and continued taking pictures. I turned to our group and proposed that we call Richard Sobol. I suggested to the others that if this person was a local law enforcement officer or FBI agent, then the government was acting illegally in intimidating and harassing us in our beliefs. Indeed, new people would refuse to join our protest if they knew that their participation was being photographed by state or federal authorities.

Tyrell, two Tulane students, and I left for the LCDC office. When we arrived Richard was in, but he did not seem particularly interested in our concerns. He was busy working on the Bogalusa civil rights cases, and he probably did not appreciate my taking the time off to join the vigil. He informed us that this was not a civil rights issue, but rather a civil liberties issue, and that we should find the local American Civil Liberties Union (ACLU) attorney. But when we demurred, arguing that we needed action right away, he grudgingly agreed to check into it.

When we reached the vigil, Richard spotted the photographer. Walking over to him, he said, "Hi, I'm Richard Sobol, who are you?" and extended his hand. "Oh, so you're Richard Sobol, good," beamed the photographer. And before Richard knew what was happening, the photographer picked up his camera, focused it, and snapped Richard's picture. Then the cameraman jotted Richard's name onto his pad.

That did it. Richard's frustration in having to assist us transformed itself into fury. He spun around, got back in his car, and drove directly to the office. He immediately drafted a complaint petitioning the local federal district court to enjoin the photographer from continuing to take pictures of the people at the vigil. The court papers also requested that all the pictures and negatives be destroyed. I drafted affidavits from several of us who had had our pictures taken, and Richard attached them to the pleadings.

Some time after filing the lawsuit, with David Bresnick's research assistance, Richard discovered that the photographer was a member of the Intelligence Division of the New Orleans police department, and that he and other officers had been taking pictures of demonstrators not only at our vigil but at other antiwar and antidraft protests and rallies in the city. But the federal district court, the local trial court, supported the police and dismissed our case. In 1971 the U.S. Court of Appeals for the Fifth Circuit issued a very brief opinion acknowledging the "competing public interest of protection of life and property of all citizens." However, it affirmed the lower court decision.[1] On balance, the court ruled, "the means and manner used by the [police officers] in photographing demonstrations did not cause any unreasonable interference with the rights of private persons to demonstrate."[2]

Our injury, of course, was nothing like the physical and personal injustices that black people suffered every day in the South. We had not been beaten, sprayed with water hoses, attacked by dogs, or even arrested. But somehow, maybe because of our white middle-class sense of entitlement, we felt an injustice had been done. We expected that our nation's law enforcement agencies would never intimidate citizens who did nothing more than stand silently in a park—and that if they did intimidate us, the courts would rectify the injustice. We were wrong.

About ten days after the Hiroshima demonstration and a week before the summer law student program was to end, we held an end-of-the-summer party at our apartment on Bourbon Street. We invited the CORE workers from Bogalusa, the law students who worked in Louisiana and Mississippi (many of the Mississippi-based students were passing through New Orleans on their way home), our friends at Tulane, and the very small local liberal community.

As the night wore on, the crowd grew, drinks flowed freely, people sang freedom songs at the top of their lungs, others danced to a blaring Rolling Stones album, some jumped into the pool fully clothed, and others tossed their clothes off—whether in the pool or out. By morning, the poolside area was littered with dissipated bodies and empty beer cans, wine bottles, crawfish heads, and oyster shells. The only distinction between this crowd and any other morning-after crowd in New Orleans was that some of the bodies on the deck that morning were black.

Later that morning, our landlady dropped off an eviction notice. At first I thought it was because we had disturbed the neighbors. But I should have realized that noise in the French Quarter, and especially on Bourbon Street, could not have been a towering concern. Rather, the landlady speculated out loud whether we were "civil rights workers" and "Commies." Moreover, she didn't want "no niggers" on her property or in her swimming pool. Since we were about to leave anyway, no one really cared about the eviction. Our summer was over in another week.

Bogalusa was still in the news. Several weeks earlier, on July 10 and 11, 150 blacks in Bogalusa had marched to Franklinton, the parish seat. The march itself took place without incident. Thirty-five state troopers protected the marchers. However, when the marchers reached

Franklinton and tried to test and integrate the local cafes, they found that all the cafes had closed for the day.

On the last day of July, Clarence Triggs, a black man from Bogalusa, was found dead near a wrecked car owned by a white woman. He had been shot in the head. Royan Burris, the vice president of the Deacons, went to the scene at 3 A.M. and was arrested for interfering with the police investigation. Royan and others believed that Triggs had been followed by two white men. The next day, the blacks in Bogalusa planned night marches to demand that the police find and arrest the killer or killers. On August 2, the police did arrest two white men, one of whom was the husband of the woman. However, the one man brought to trial was acquitted by an all-white jury, and no one else was ever prosecuted for the crime.

It was time to leave. But I was not ready to return to New York; I needed a transition. Tyrell Collins, two Tulane students, and I arranged to drive a rental car to Chicago. The others were going to visit family. I planned to visit a high school friend who had moved there. But my real incentive for driving to Chicago was to travel through the heartland of Louisiana and up into Mississippi. It seemed an adventurous, although possibly perilous, way to end the summer.

The day before we left, Henry Austin decided to join us. Henry was twenty-two, a tall, thin, young black man from Baton Rouge with a Choctaw Indian bloodline (many blacks in Louisiana claimed Indian ancestry) whose name inspired hatred throughout the white community in Bogalusa. In July 1965, Henry had shot a white man in Bogalusa. The incident occurred when he and another black man, Milton Johnson, were driving behind approximately four hundred black marchers protesting the job discrimination at Crown Zellerbach and other local businesses, discrimination against black customers at local cafes, and the recent killing of a black deputy sheriff. Henry and Milton were providing backup in case a demonstrator was injured and needed to be taken to a clinic or hospital.

The deputy sheriff had been killed a month before Henry's shooting incident. The parish's first two black deputies, hired only a year before, were ambushed as they drove their patrol car in the town of Varnado, seven miles north of Bogalusa. Deputy O'Neal Moore, the driver, died from a rifle shot to the head. His partner, Creed Rogers, lost his right eye to a shotgun blast. A witness reported seeing a pickup truck following the police vehicle. Because different guns were used in the shootings, the police surmised that there were at least three people riding in the truck.

Ennis Ray McElveen, a white man who owned the truck and who worked for Crown Zellerbach in Bogalusa, but who lived in Mississippi, was arrested for the murder. But neither McElveen nor anyone else was ever convicted. McElveen was a member of the White Citizens Council and the National States Rights Party, which the *New York Times* had described as a "right-wing, anti-Semite, racist organization."[3]

J. B. Stoner, an attorney for the States Rights Party, had visited Bogalusa several times to whip up racist white frenzy.* He returned in July 1965 to lead a counterprotest against the black marchers. Speaking to a crowd of over two thousand whites, Stoner said, "The nigger is not a human being. He is somewhere between the white man and the ape. . . .We don't believe in tolerance. We don't believe in getting along with our enemy, and the nigger is our enemy. . . .What the nigger really wants is our white women."[4]

It was during this week of protests by the black demonstrators and the counterprotests by Stoner and white demonstrators that Henry shot his white assailant. With Milton Johnson driving and Henry sitting in the passenger seat of A. Z. Young's 1964 Cadillac taxi (A. Z. owned a cab company), they followed behind the marchers. Suddenly, Hattie Mae Hill, a seventeen-year-old black marcher, was struck in the head by a bottle. Blood flowing from her wound, she ran to Leneva Tiebeman, a white nurse and a member of the medical committee on human rights.

---

* James Earl Ray, the convicted assassin of Martin Luther King, hired J. B. Stoner to represent him in seeking a hearing to overturn his guilty plea.

Leneva pushed Hattie Mae into Henry and Milton's car and fell on top of her.

Henry was looking out the driver's side window when Alton Crowe, a white man from the neighboring town of Pearl River, walked up to the car with several other men and started pummeling Henry and Milton. Henry pulled out his pistol and shot Crowe in the chest and the neck. Crowe was in critical condition but survived.[5]

Henry was arrested and put on $25,000 bond. Henry indicated to the press that he was a member of the Deacons and had been at the march to protect the black demonstrators.* Since Henry's actions could easily have been interpreted as self-defense, and since the city of Bogalusa did not want the negative publicity, much less the possibility of further violent demonstrations accompanying a trial, the city's white leaders forged an understanding with the black community: if Henry stayed out of Bogalusa, the district attorney would not prosecute.

During the following years, Henry maintained the fiction that he had not returned to Bogalusa. Many local black leaders saw Henry as a meddlesome outsider and a hothead and did not want him around. But in fact he often surfaced in the city's black neighborhoods. When Henry was not hiding out in Bogalusa, he was usually in New Orleans, passing time at the CORE office.

Because Henry was smart, a civil rights group arranged for him to receive a scholarship to attend Antioch College in Yellow Springs, Ohio. Henry left for Chicago and points north that summer of 1966 with us, but he returned soon thereafter.

I met up with Henry again in the summer of 1967, spending time with him both in New Orleans and in Bogalusa. Whenever we walked together in the French Quarter, the police stopped us and demanded identification. Perhaps they recognized Henry, although I doubt that is

---

* Bob Hicks told me that Henry, who was from Baton Rouge, was never a member of the Deacons (interview on April 28, 1997).

why they accosted us. The sight of a black man and a white man walking together was reason enough.

In one of my most moving experiences that summer, Henry told how he could not leave Louisiana. We were sitting with Michael Millemann, another law student, by the bank of the river in the French Quarter. As we watched the ships navigate the sometimes treacherous bends, Henry, his face drawn, expressed his longings. He was barred from returning to Bogalusa, his adopted home, on penalty of a long prison sentence. Sure, he had opportunities up north, but his heart was in Louisiana. There was work to be done in Bogalusa, and he could not run away from it.

Then his thoughts shifted to us. Mirroring the words of D'Army Bailey during my 1966 orientation outside Jackson, Henry compared my view of the world, and Michael's, to his own perspective. We could return to our homes any time and leave the South behind. We could, and would, move on in law school and in our professions. But there was no escape for Henry Austin. He saw himself as a trapped animal, snared "whether I stay in Louisiana or leave for Ohio." He could never transcend his black skin or his circumstances. Once again I was reminded how different it was to be born white and grow up in the North—and how many things I took for granted.

I can still picture our band driving through northern Louisiana on our way to Chicago, looking up at the low, ashen sky and watching it clear into breathtaking pinks, yellows, oranges, and reds as the sunset painted its colors somewhere near the Mississippi border. Henry remarked that nowhere in the country was the sky so brilliant, but Tyrell corrected him. California too had psychedelic sunsets, she said.

Crossing into Mississippi that night gave me the creeps. I kept remembering Chaney, Goodman, and Schwerner, stopped by local sheriffs in Philadelphia, summarily executed, and buried beneath tons of rubble. The others in the car must have been thinking along the same lines, since each of us prayed to God or meditated in our own ways that our car would not break down.

We sang freedom songs—"We Shall Overcome," "Keep Your Hands on the Plow," and "Ain't Gonna Let Nobody Turn Me Around"—to distract ourselves. We crooned rock and roll: "You Can't Hurry Love," "Knock on Wood," and "Mustang Sally." And we shared memories of the summer and of past times to crowd out the ghosts and our fears. Other times, we were quiet, and the dark shadows outside invaded the silence. When we stopped for gas, Henry stayed in the car so we wouldn't attract attention as a mixed-race group.

Hours later, we made it. We were all still wide awake when we drove across the Mississippi border into Memphis, Tennessee. But I could not truly relax until we crossed through Tennessee and Kentucky and pulled into Cairo, Illinois. Cairo, the southernmost city in Illinois, had lots of Southern old-boy influences. In fact, in the summer of 1967, the National Guard was called in to stem racial unrest when blacks demanded more employment opportunities. But it was in Illinois, and somehow that signified the North and safety to me.

When I left Louisiana that August, I knew I would return the following summer. My three months in the South had been exhilarating, and I wanted more. But events that fall in New Orleans, along with LCDC's incursion into white supremacist Leander Perez's Plaquemines Parish, summoned me to Louisiana sooner than that. I was back in LCDC's offices by December.

That winter introduced me to an entirely new Louisiana. Plaquemines Parish was only sixty miles farther south, nestled between New Orleans and the Gulf of Mexico. But as a society it was in the dark ages. The black residents were so psychologically beaten down that no one even thought of raising a hand in opposition. If Bogalusa represented a triumph of the Louisiana civil rights movement, Plaquemines Parish was the nadir.

TEN

Slave Quarters
on Royal Street

When David Bresnick and I returned to New York in the fall of 1966, we talked about creating a newsletter that would identify the projects that law students were working on and encourage students to reflect on the rise of Black Power, the significance of the antiwar movement, and the overall direction and future of civil rights activity in both the North and the South. We convinced the Law Students Civil Rights Research Council to fund the newsletter, and the first edition of *LSCRRC* appeared in December 1966. In our opening article we proclaimed our goal: "vindication of civil rights" through an "open-ended . . . confrontation of the issues." Writing and editing the newsletter was instructive. As I chronicled other students' voices as well as my own, I had the opportunity to reexamine our lives in those heady days. But writing could not substitute for action, and I was anxious to return south.

Late that December I flew back down to New Orleans. The Lawyers Constitutional Defense Committee paid for the flight and put me up at 932 Royal Street, a flat owned by LCDC. It was a perfect opportunity: Richard Sobol needed law student assistance in the winter months in Bogalusa and Plaquemines Parish, and I was eager to return. The offer was so much more satisfying than going to school that I did not return to NYU when classes began in the new year but stayed in Louisiana until the middle of February.

For the most part, I found law school classes dreary and unreal compared to what I was doing in Louisiana. Even the civil rights classes I was taking—and New York University offered more classes on civil rights and civil liberties law than any other school in the country—could not match my firsthand experiences of the summer. Besides, with its relatively professional and conservative demeanor, to my mind, the school still had a long way to go. And to the extent that I was missing anything at all in my classes, I wasn't worried. I was great at cramming.

The flat on Royal Street was in the back of a two-story building in what was called the "Slave Quarters." How authentic that designation made me feel. I loved climbing the rickety wooden steps to what was to be my home for the next eight weeks. Across the street someone had built a remarkable wrought-iron fence of cornstalks entwined with morning glories; thirty years later, the fence is part of the Cornstalk Fence Hotel.

Royal Street was very different from Bourbon Street. There were no naked ladies grinding and bumping in windows or foul-mouthed, repulsive barkers enticing passersby into their lairs. On Royal the tourists came to find the reminders of an era crumbling underfoot but still clung to by the Southern gentry: overstuffed Victorian chairs, ornate tables and inlaid desks; muskets and ammunition from the Civil War; and, of course, used books by English and Southern poets and writers. It was the street of antique shops and art galleries and of cast-iron horse-head hitching posts.

Down a ways on Royal stood the old courthouse, with its marble staircases, marble hallways, stained-glass skylights, brass chandeliers, and seventeen-foot ceilings. At one time it was home to the Federal District Court and the Federal Court of Appeals; at another time it housed the Louisiana State Supreme Court. Often I would do my research in the semicircular rooms of the court library, its windows overlooking the Mississippi River on one side and the French Quarter on the other. Once, when I had to work late, one of the librarians—who was also the niece of a justice of the Louisiana Supreme Court—allowed me to remain in the library and close up the building on my own. Perhaps she felt that anyone associated with the law—even a New Yorker—was trustworthy. Or maybe she did not think that there was anything to steal, although I did have access to all the back rooms, including the judges' chambers. I don't think she ever knew that I did civil rights work. She never asked. And I am not sure it would have made a difference to her, even though most of our cases opposed the views of her uncle and a majority of the members of the court. I suspect that when it came down to it, Southern hospitality was so ingrained in that upper crust of New Orleans society that she couldn't help but be supremely accommodating and gracious.

Late one afternoon I was on my way back to the office on Dryades Street from the library when I heard the sounds of trombones, trumpets, a saxophone, and drums. I ran to the corner of Jackson in time to see a parade of black men and women in white shirts and black pants or skirts playing and dancing to traditional jazz. The leader of the makeshift band wore a black jacket and carried a baton. It was a jazz funeral, and they were returning from the cemetery. A woman hiked her skirt and twirled about as the band began a rousing rendition of "When the Saints Come Marching In." Down the street, outside a home on Jackson, people were preparing a spread of fried chicken, cornbread, and potato salad. I fell in behind the marchers to join the joyous noise. As the crowd grew larger and larger, I recalled words that I had read not long before, words that summed up the spirit of jazz funerals: "Cry when you enter the world, rejoice when you leave."

If I walked a block or two up from my Royal Street home toward Canal Street and then turned the corner on either St. Peter or St. Ann, walking over to Chartres, I reached Jackson Square. On those serene, mild winter evenings, I sat in the park and savored deep-fried cannoli filled with chocolate, vanilla, or strawberry ice cream from the Italian cafe on the square. Babe Stovall, one of the street musicians who played folk or jazz tunes on beat-up guitars and drums and funky handmade whistles and mouth organs, sang the blues to us in the park. I purchased his record from him and played it often, wondering why he had not been "discovered."

The most famous edifice in the Quarter loomed over the park and the square—St. Louis Cathedral. An earlier cathedral had been constructed on this spot in 1724, but it had been destroyed. The new cathedral was built between 1849 and 1851. (In September 1987 Pope John Paul II celebrated High Mass in the sanctuary, blessing the church and congregation.) To an outsider, New Orleans is strongly beholden to its French Catholic heritage. But in early 1967, as I watched the Mardi Gras festivities and parades, I made a surprising, actually shocking, discovery: it wasn't the Catholics but the Protestants, the WASPs, who dominated the local culture and perhaps the politics. And although the media had led me to believe that Mardi Gras was a grand time, I saw very little of its festive side. To this intense and earnest civil rights activist, the festivities were smoke and mirrors, concealing a racist and classist landscape. But before I was to peek behind the beguiling mask of Mardi Gras, I needed to travel to the bayous of Plaquemines Parish and assist Richard Sobol in the Gary Duncan case.

ELEVEN

An Unwarranted Touching

Plaquemines Parish was infamous among civil rights workers as the fief-dom of Leander H. Perez. He was a short, stocky man, although his signature pompadour added several inches to his height. By creating dummy corporations to control the parish's oil and sulfur fields, Perez had become the richest and most powerful person in the parish. He began practicing law in 1914 and was elected parish judge from 1920 to 1924. He served as the parish district attorney from 1924 until 1960, when, in regal style, he bequeathed the post to his son, Leander Perez Jr. After he resigned his district attorney post, the elder Perez created the Plaquemines Parish Commission Council as the governing body of the parish, then persuaded the council to elect him president. As such he continued to dominate the parish's political scene. Since the population of the parish was only twenty-five thousand, Perez was the meta-phorical big fish in a small pond for more than half a century.

In 1954 Perez helped organize the White Citizens Councils, the front organizations for the Ku Klux Klan. Perez once told an audience of White Citizens Council members that they must act against the blacks soon, before "these Congolese rape your daughters."[1] However, his prejudices transcended color: as early as 1960, Perez charged that Communists and "Zionist Jews" were behind the civil rights movement.[2]

Perez loved to broadcast his purchase of an isolated eighteenth-century Spanish fort on the Mississippi River, known as Fort St. Philip, surrounded by a moat. In 1964 he declared that if any civil rights workers, particularly CORE workers, were foolish enough to enter Plaquemines Parish, they would be confined in the fort or tossed into the alligator-packed moat, never to be heard from again. He also memorably observed, "We're not near ready to surrender our peaceful, beautiful parish to the Communists. And if Martin Luther King comes in, we'll guarantee his transportation across the [Mississippi] river—part way, that is."[3]

Perez was excommunicated from the Catholic Church in 1962 for his rabid opposition to the desegregation of diocesan and public schools. He boasted to the archbishop, "If you think you can send me to hell, I'll ask you to go to hell."[4] (However, after Perez died in 1969 a spokesperson for the church announced that in 1968 Perez had made a conciliatory speech that led to the lifting of the excommunication order.) In 1965, at the time of the passage of the Voting Rights Act, only 96 of the 6,500 African Americans in the parish were registered to vote. That year, federal registrars came into the parish and registered another 2,000 blacks.

The Plaquemines Parish case I worked on started innocently enough. In fall 1966 the local schools had been ordered by the federal court to integrate. Gary Duncan, a nineteen-year-old black man, married with a new baby, was concerned about the safety of a cousin and a nephew who had enrolled in the formerly all-white high school. After hearing of harassment of the black students, Gary decided to swing by one afternoon. On October 18, 1966, Gary spotted his nephew and cousin in some sort of confrontation with four white boys outside the school. Several white men were also "observing" the scene. Gary stopped to see what was going on. Gary's nephew and cousin told him that the white boys wanted to start a fight with them.

Gary Duncan spoke with the white boys and then told his cousin and nephew to get in the car. Gary then allegedly touched one of the white boys before he himself got into the car and drove away. One of the white men observing the scene, the president of the local private school association created in response to the desegregation order, called the sheriff's office. Several minutes later, a deputy sheriff stopped Gary's car and returned with him to the scene of the incident. But after interviewing the white boys and examining the boy who said that he had been struck, the deputy said that he did not believe that Gary had struck the boy and released him.

However, after hearing about the incident three days later, Leander Perez Jr., the local district attorney, arrested Gary Duncan. Richard Haley, the Southern director for CORE, told Gary Duncan's parents about Richard Sobol and LCDC, and they set up an appointment. After meeting with Gary and his cousin and nephew, Richard agreed to take the case. It was not the kind of case that LCDC usually took—that is, a case arising out of a civil rights demonstration, so common in Bogalusa. But to Richard it was not a simple criminal case, either. It was another form of intimidation of African Americans who dared to stand up for their rights—this time, the right of Gary's nephew and cousin to attend an integrated school free of harassment.

Originally the charge against Gary Duncan was "cruelty to juveniles." But when Richard Sobol explained to the court and the assistant district attorney that the charge applied only to people who had parental or supervisory control over a child, the district attorney recharged Gary Duncan with simple battery, an unwarranted touching.

As expected, the testimony at trial was in dispute. The white boys testified that Gary slapped the white boy on the elbow before getting in the car. Gary's cousin and nephew testified that Gary did not slap the boy but had merely touched him. Although the sheriff's deputy had agreed with Gary's relatives, the trial judge, to no one's surprise, embraced the testimony of the white boys. The judge was Eugene Leon, one of the many persons in Plaquemines Parish who owed their jobs to Leander Perez Sr. Lolis Elie had known Leon in law school at Loyola, and, as Lolis tells it, Leon was quite civil to him. But that relationship changed in 1966 when Perez selected Leon as his candidate for the local judgeship and Leon had to demonstrate his undivided loyalty to Perez.

Before the trial began, Richard Sobol had requested that the case be heard before a jury. Leon denied the request. Under the Louisiana constitution, jury trials were only available in cases where the defendant could be sentenced to death or to imprisonment at hard labor. Simple battery was defined as a misdemeanor with a maximum possible sentence of two years' imprisonment, not at hard labor, and a $300 fine. Although Richard's first priority was to obtain an acquittal for Gary, he knew that if Gary were convicted he would have to find grounds for an appeal. His strongest argument would be that by denying Gary a trial before a jury, the Louisiana justice system deprived Gary of his right to a fundamentally fair trial.

In 1967, each state was free to determine its own criteria for jury trials in criminal proceedings. However, every state save Louisiana did afford the right whenever a defendant was charged with a crime that attached a prison sentence of longer than one year. And only two states unequivocally denied jury trials for crimes punishable by more than six months' imprisonment: New York City provided jury trials only for crimes bearing maximum sentences of greater than one year, and New Jersey's disorderly conduct statute carried a one-year maximum sentence without a jury trial. Ten other states provided penalties of over six months without jury trials at the initial stage. But a defendant who was convicted had the right to request a new trial before a jury.

When I researched the Louisiana statutes, I found that the crime of simple battery was not the only one for which a defendant could be denied a jury trial and receive a lengthy prison sentence. Louisiana had a number of criminal statutes that did not allow for jury trials, including an extreme situation whereby a person could receive up to ten years in prison without a jury trial for the crime of aggravated battery resulting from breach of the peace. Another statute provided up to three years in prison without a jury trial for the crime of wearing a mask in public at any time other than Mardi Gras.

The framers of the United States Constitution and the constitutions of the forty-nine other states modeled their laws on the English legal system, in which the right to a jury trial dated back to the Magna Carta. Because of its French heritage, Louisiana instead patterned many of its laws on the French civil law and court system. Under French civil law, and under Louisiana law, a trial before one's peers was not seen as a fundamental right.

During the 1950s and 1960s the U.S. Supreme Court, under Earl Warren, had taken a broad brush to the Constitution, expanding many of the rights and protections provided in the Bill of Rights. Although the Bill of Rights applied to federal government employees and proceedings, the Warren Court ruled that the due process and equal protection clauses of the Fourteenth Amendment extended several rights in the Bill of Rights to the actions of state government employees and to state court proceedings. The rights to freedom of speech, press, and religion under the First Amendment, the right to freedom from unreasonable searches and seizures under the Fourth Amendment, the right to freedom from compelled self-incrimination under the Fifth Amendment, and the right to an attorney under the Sixth Amendment were all adopted as part of the Court's expansionary decision-making.

The right to a jury trial in a federal criminal case has always been protected under the Sixth Amendment, which reads: "In all criminal prosecutions, the accused shall enjoy the right to a speedy trial and public trial, by an impartial jury of the State and district wherein the crime shall have been committed."

As expected, Judge Leon found Gary Duncan guilty of simple battery and set sentencing for one week later. The argument that Richard planned to make on appeal was that by not permitting jury trials except in very serious cases, Louisiana was denying its citizens a fundamental right guaranteed in the Sixth Amendment and one that should also be extended to people in state trials and proceedings through the due process clause in the Fourteenth Amendment. Ultimately, Richard secured the chance to make that argument before the Supreme Court in the landmark case of *Duncan v Louisiana*.

TWELVE

Louisiana Justice

I did not attend the Duncan trial on January 25, 1967; I needed to be in Bogalusa. But I did drive down with Richard Sobol to the courthouse in Pointe-à-la-Hache, Plaquemines Parish, on sentencing day, February 1.

Much of Plaquemines Parish lies below sea level. Two roads parallel the Mississippi River, one on each bank. Pointe-à-la-Hache, on the eastern bank, looked like a hatchet point on old maps, hence its name. To reach it from the western side of the Mississippi, you need to take a three-minute ferry ride. In the spring of 1997, while I waited for the ferry, I spotted the words "Blacks Demand Justice" scrawled in black lettering on the metal siding that partially sheltered the uninviting waiting area. I guess some things have changed. Thirty years ago, blacks in the parish also wanted justice, but they were too cowed by Leander Perez and his henchmen to demand it publicly.

Much of the drive to the parish courthouse that day in 1967 was through low swamp country and salt marsh. The river was channeled by levees. The land was marked with cottonwood, live oaks cradling Spanish moss, saw grass, and sugarcane. Cypress trees (the dead ones, eerily hollow and barren of leaves and color) and cypress knees (which provided part of the living trees' root-breathing system) reached out of the pea-green bayou waters. The only signs of human habitation were the clapboard cafes selling ice-cold beer, whitewashed concrete gas stations, crushed cans strewn along the road, aluminum-clad trailer homes perched on cinder blocks or wooden stilts—mimicking the long-legged egrets and herons standing in the mucky waters—and the weather-beaten pirogues and motorboats meandering through the swamps. Signs of other life were bountiful, though. The bayou was home to great blue herons, snowy egrets, alligators and turtles sunning themselves on logs, ospreys circling overhead, ravens, mockingbirds, rabbits, and an armadillo road kill. The feeling I had that day was one of dreadful loneliness in phantom, though hauntingly beautiful, terrain. Neither Richard nor I said much.

I was relieved when we arrived at the yellow and red brick and stucco courthouse at Pointe-à-la-Hache, even when I spotted the Confederate flag prominently displayed on one side of the building. At least we were now in a town, I thought. But New York City it wasn't: the only urban amenities were a market, built from concrete blocks and painted forest green, and a bail bondsman's office. And whatever sense of security I felt was quickly dispelled when my eyes lit on the signs marking "white" and "colored" restrooms. Three years after the passing of the Civil Rights Act of 1964, Pointe-à-la-Hache remained immune to federal injunctions.

Richard and I took seats in the public section of the courtroom. We were early, and other court matters preceded Gary Duncan's sentencing. It was a small courtroom; we sat opposite Judge Leon's elevated, oak-paneled bench. As I sat down, I let my mind wander, thinking that not much would happen until our case was called. I felt only a modicum of interest in the first case of the day.

The matter concerned a skinny, pasty-faced white man who had been accused of statutory rape: that is, intercourse with a person under seventeen. He was wearing a tropical-weight brown suit. His wife, wearing a wide-brimmed hat, and his two daughters, about ten and twelve, sat in front of us. When the bailiff called his name, the defendant stood up.

"How do you plead?" asked the judge, his pinkish-white mouth tracing a smile as he spoke to the defendant. Before the defendant could answer, two lawyers, one on either side of the defendant, rose. "If Your Honor would be so kind as to allow, we request some additional time to research this matter before we make our plea," answered one.

"How much time do you need?" asked Judge Leon.

"About two or three more weeks, Your Honor."

"Three weeks it is," pronounced the judge.

"Thank you, Your Honor," responded the attorney. Then all three men, the defendant and his two attorneys, walked out. The wife and girls followed, their eyes firmly fixed on the floor.

"Next case!" ordered the judge.

The next defendant brought into the room was a brawny man, with skin the color of shiny black silk. He appeared to be in his mid-twenties. He stood up, focusing his eyes on the floor and keeping his weathered hands to his sides. His ankles were chained together. The charges were read: he was accused of rape.

"Do you have an attorney?" the judge demanded.

"I am his court-appointed attorney, Your Honor," bellowed a burly white man who had been sitting at the counsel table near the judge's bench. We watched as he struggled to extricate himself from his seat and stand more or less upright. He leaned his palms on the table for balance. Was he drunk that early in the morning, I wondered, or was it his considerable bulk that caused him to sway and lean so?

"And how does he plead?" asked the judge.

"He pleads guilty, Your Honor," drawled the attorney.

Without a moment's delay, the judge issued the sentence. "Fourteen years' imprisonment at hard labor. Bailiff, take him away."

The defendant raised his hands to the bailiff to be handcuffed, and, taking imprecise steps, moved toward the door. The bailiff led him to a waiting deputy sheriff's car. All his mannerisms spoke of a spirit broken years before. As the bailiff led the defendant away, the white lawyer released his grip on the table and slumped back into his seat. I couldn't tell whether he needed to rest before leaving the courtroom or whether he was waiting to "represent" another defendant.

In law school, we were being taught that the legal system was in a glorious progressive stage. Under Earl Warren's stewardship, the Supreme Court was fiercely establishing and protecting individual rights. People once victimized by the legal system could now take their complaints to the Court, where they would be heard and redressed. Lawyers truly were making a difference.

My law school professors were especially approving of the decision in *Gideon v Wainwright*, the 1963 case that established the right to an attorney in most criminal proceedings. The compelling story of Clarence Gideon's belief in the right to counsel was told in *Gideon's Trumpet*, by the *New York Times* reporter Anthony Lewis. It captured the sense of hope and fulfillment of the 1960s. It inspired me then and still does today. Yet the words I heard in law school and the words I had read in Lewis's book took on new meaning that day in Plaquemines Parish. Yes, everyone now had the right to an attorney. But who would make sure that an unsophisticated defendant would be given that right in a meaningful way? And who was to protect the defendant from his own attorney? What did the right to representation really mean here in the backwoods of Louisiana? Or, for that matter, in the streets of New York? In Plaquemines Parish it was obvious that class and money protected your rights considerably better than any edicts from nine people in black robes.

Of course, it was possible, even likely, that the black defendant's attorney had struck a plea bargain deal with the prosecution prior to the sentencing. But I doubt that the defendant's guilt was a major factor. In the 1960s South, black defendants knew the harsh reality of a trial: the entrenched white judiciary taking its cue from the local white prosecutors would find African Americans guilty regardless of the actual evidence.

I had no idea whether the punishment was commensurate with the crime, since I knew nothing more about the alleged rape. I wanted to know whether the woman whom he was accused of raping was white or black. Probably not black, I reasoned, since the white-dominated justice system often did not bother to prosecute crimes of black against black. If she had been white, I thought, the sentence probably would have been death. But perhaps he never did rape her, and the plea bargain was the best he could escape with for the crime of being found in the company of a white woman in a segregated society.

The spirit of the law changed for me that day. I had crossed another borderline.

Our case was next: *State of Louisiana v Gary Duncan*. We had met Gary outside the courthouse. He had been out on bail since being found guilty of simple battery a week before. Gary was still a teenager, although his soft brown eyes spoke of a much older man. He was about five feet ten inches tall, of medium build, but muscles rippled through his white T-shirt. He spoke little but shook our hands warmly. Gary's mother and wife stood at his side. Richard sat with Gary up front at the counsel table, while I sat with Gary's family in the spectator section.

When the case was called, Judge Leon asked the defendant to rise. Richard rose with him. Leon imposed a sentence of sixty days in prison and a $150 fine.

Richard Sobol then informed Judge Leon that he would appeal to the Louisiana Supreme Court on the basis of the judge's denial of his request for a jury trial. Judge Leon set bond at $1,500 pending the appeal. Gary was handcuffed and taken off to prison. Gary's wife and mother tried to reach him to say their good-byes, but they were blocked by the bailiff. Before they reached the front of the courtroom, Gary had been ushered out the door and into a waiting police van.

Richard tried to reassure Gary's family by saying that he believed that the sheriffs and prison staff wouldn't harm Gary, since too many civil rights people were watching. It was little consolation. Gary had done nothing wrong and yet had been sentenced to two months in a Louisiana prison. Gary's wife mulled aloud about what sentence Gary might have received if Richard and other civil rights people had not been involved in his representation. Would Judge Leon have been easier on him if Gary had been contrite and a "good nigger"? Was he being sentenced so harshly because of his associations? Or would it have been just the opposite? Would Leon have wanted to teach Gary a lesson for being an "uppity nigger," for talking to and touching a white boy, and given him an even stiffer sentence?

As soon as the sentencing was over, we said our good-byes to Gary's wife and mother and raced to the car. Richard was still nervous that something could happen to us, and his anxiety was contagious. I flashed on the character of Atticus Finch in *To Kill a Mockingbird* (played by Gregory Peck in the movie). While Finch was preparing to appeal Tom Robinson's conviction, the local whites were preparing a lynching party. Richard was not sure what might happen, but both Perez Sr. and Perez Jr. had made it clear they didn't want any outside agitators on their turf. Richard did not care to overstay his welcome. On that trip, we made it back safely. Richard was not so lucky nearly three weeks later when he drove up to Plaquemines Parish alone.

THIRTEEN

Jailhouse Fears

One February day, at three in the afternoon, A. Z. Young called LCDC from Bogalusa. Once again picketers outside the businesses on Columbia Road had been arrested. A mob of whites had attacked them with clubs, and the Deacons had rushed in to protect the demonstrators. The black demonstrators had been arrested for "refusing to disperse." A. Z. asked us to come to Bogalusa to interview those arrested and to bail them out. Richard was busy on the *Duncan* case, and Don Juneau, LCDC's newly hired associate, was out of the office researching some issues at the courthouse. Richard said I had to go.

Don Juneau was the first LCDC lawyer licensed to practice in Louisiana. Don was a native, born in Alexandria, the heart of the Cajun culture, and bred in Hammond, about forty miles north of New Orleans. He attended boarding school in Covington, across Lake Pontchartrain from New Orleans and on the road to Bogalusa. When I first met Don, I wondered what it was that made him withdraw from and ultimately work against the racist system in which he had been raised. Don credits the many books he read as a kid for opening his eyes to other worlds. But it was *Black Boy* by Richard Wright, which he read at the age of eleven, that made an enduring impression on him.

Don's family, too, was more progressive than many in the South. He recalled that one day, when Don and his friend were playing, the friend called the Juneau's family maid a "nigger." Don's parents, who had overheard the remark, said nothing directly—that was not the Southern way. But it was understood that Don was never to invite that friend over again.

Don went to the University of Southwest Louisiana in Lafayette and Tulane Law School in New Orleans. Between college and law school, he acquired a master's degree in philosophy at Georgetown. The first time I met him, Don was sitting at a desk by the storefront window in the LCDC office. As I walked in, he looked up, greeted me, and in the same breath implored me to sit down and admire his new fountain pen. For the next ten minutes, he explained its intricacies, strokes, and history. He lamented its imminent departure from our lives—to be replaced by the graceless, soulless ballpoint. I was not all that interested in fountain pens, but I sat transfixed. Then, without pausing, Don launched into a story concerning some event in the Civil War. To this day, I cannot say how he made the leap from fountain pen to Civil War. But it really didn't matter. Don Juneau was a storyteller, and his inquisitive mind knew no bounds as it pounced from one account or anecdote to another. As long as the listener remained attentive, Don had an absorbing narrative to tell. I was always an appreciative listener.

For my trip to Bogalusa, I called Avis to reserve a car. Then I called A.Z. Young and told him that I would arrive around five o'clock. A.Z. said that two armed Deacon cars would be waiting to escort me into town.

The pickets in Bogalusa had continued nearly every day for more than a year, and the white-owned businesses were suffering. During the previous Christmas season, they had been so frustrated at the success of the boycott that they called in the local Klan to break up the demonstrations. The Klansmen were only too willing to comply. Of course, the Deacons for Defense and Justice were also standing by, ready for action. So, at times, all hell broke loose. White police officers were always present to "maintain order," and although they were still under court order to protect the blacks, they often turned their heads when whites beat up black demonstrators. Richard Sobol regularly filed complaints in federal court that the white police officers were not discharging their duties to protect the picketers.

The demonstrators were still in jail when I arrived at the Bogalusa jailhouse before six that evening. I crossed through the outside door and then walked through the jail doorway—an imposing steel door with metal netting layered against a window. The walls of the narrow corridor were painted a dull gray, a gray that was disturbed by the bright red "STOP" sign and the words "No weapons allowed in Jail" painted in green. At the door the sheriff received me graciously.

"Welcome, counselor," he said, his fleshy hand stuck out to me. Wearing a Stetson hat that covered his thick black eyebrows, he was dressed in a blue work shirt, blue jeans, and cowboy boots. "I assume you are the lawyer for the demonstrators arrested. Would you like to see them now?" He was smiling. I couldn't tell whether he was truly charming by nature or whether he was afraid that if things did not go smoothly, LCDC would once again be on the phone with federal agencies requesting investigations by the FBI, the U.S. Civil Rights Commission, and the Justice Department. Or perhaps he figured that the more gracious he was, the faster I would be out of there.

I was wearing a brown, lightweight cotton jacket and a brown knitted tie. Perhaps I looked like a lawyer. But I was twenty-two years old, too young to be a member of the bar. I was sure I looked my age or younger, certainly not older. So why was the sheriff calling me "counselor"? Was this a trick?

The law was very clear. Practicing law without a license was a serious crime. If I were arrested, I could spend time in jail without much hope that the federal courts would overturn my state trial on discriminatory grounds. There was no obvious race or civil rights issue involved, as there would be if I were arrested for testing or integrating a cafe or a beach. I nodded anyway.

The sheriff looked at me and said, "As soon as you complete your interview with the demonstrators, we'll release them."

"Why do you need to wait until I finish interviewing?" I asked.

"Those were the instructions we were given. We wanted you to see how well we treat them while in jail."

It seemed odd that the sheriff would confide this to me, but it rang true. No doubt they were concerned about lawyers returning to federal court the next day to request further sanctions against them. They wanted to be sure we wouldn't be able to accuse the police and sheriffs of beating their prisoners. I was there to serve their purposes: to document that their prisoners were treated well. So while I was sweating that they would arrest me, they were sweating that I would accuse them of mistreating the prisoners. We each had our fears, I realized, although they were too preoccupied with theirs to have a glimmer of mine. I nodded again.

If I was going to interview the prisoners, I had to do it while they were in jail. But there was still one slight problem: only lawyers were permitted in the jail cells. I drifted into a disassociated state where I became two people: one of me was entering the jailhouse masquerading as a lawyer, the other was lingering at the doorway surveying the scene. As the sheriff led me down the corridors of the jail, passing open doors to supervisors' offices, I could feel the sweat collecting on my forehead and under my arms. At any moment, I could be locked up along with my "clients." We climbed a flight of metal stairs and passed through the heavy steel door separating the prisoners from the offices.

"Peter, Peter!" Gayle Jenkins had seen me coming and was calling. "Bail us out, we need to go home." The others picked up the chant. "Hey Peter, bail us out of here. We should be home with our kids." My eyes ran down the corridor over the twelve people who had been arrested that afternoon. They were crowded four to a cell. I called out, "I'm coming, Gayle. You're first." Several prisoners whooped it up. The sheriff said nothing.

After I completed my interviews with Gayle, Robert Hicks, and several other demonstrators, including two who had been injured, I turned to leave. I had spent approximately an hour in the jail. My shirt was soaked all the way through, and it wasn't from the heat. I was certain the sheriff would notice as he came up to me. But he had his own concerns.

"Have you finished interviewing your clients?" he asked. "If so, and if you would like, we can release them on bond now." Again he reminded me, "We just wanted to keep them here until you arrived and had met with them."

"Yes," I heard myself say, "release them immediately. I've completed my interviews and they must be bailed out as soon as possible. I expect all of them to be back in their homes by the time I return to New Orleans."

"They will, absolutely, counselor," he assured me. I thanked him, called back to Gayle to tell her the news, and slowly, anxiously, returned to my car. I still expected the sheriff to reappear and put me under arrest. But it never happened.

I drove over to Gayle's house. While Gayle, Robert, A. Z., and others waited with me for other people to arrive, Gayle's daughter went into the kitchen to cook up some fried eggs, grits, biscuits, and a huge pot of hot coffee. We laughed heartily while waiting for the food, chatting about the afternoon demonstration and arrests and the scene at the jail. I stayed over, sleeping as usual on the couch in the living room.

I rose early the next morning so I could get to the LCDC office before Richard arrived. I had slept poorly, still worrying whether the sheriff would show up to arrest me—although I took comfort in the fact that he probably would not expect to find me anywhere this side of Border Street.

On my way back to New Orleans, I rehearsed the speech I would make to Richard. "I need to leave the state. If they figure out that I'm not a lawyer, they'll come and arrest me. And I am definitely never going back to Bogalusa. That's it. I'm off for New York." But when I arrived back at the office at around ten that morning, I had no time to give my talk. Too many things were happening. Gayle was on the phone with Don Juneau confirming details of the arrests and injuries. Richard and Don were in high gear preparing their petition for sanctions against the

Bogalusa police and the local sheriff's department for once again violating the federal court injunction by allowing whites to attack black demonstrators. Richard wanted to file the petition that morning, adding the affidavits in support later. He directed me to draft the affidavits of the key players based on the facts I had obtained the day before. He also said that someone, probably me, would have to return to Bogalusa in the early afternoon to get the demonstrators to confirm and sign the affidavits. We would file the affidavits later that day or early the next morning.

Since I still had the rented car, and since no one else was going to drive to Bogalusa, I called up Gayle Jenkins and told her that I would be back at the outskirts of town in two hours. As usual, the Deacons were waiting. When we pulled into her driveway, Gayle was standing outside. Yesterday's demonstrators were sitting inside her home. Gayle had made sure that they would be there when I arrived. The mood was jubilant. We were winning. White businessmen were hurting, and the police feared further intrusion by the federal government.

Later that evening, when I went to bed, I thought again of the previous day's experience. I could now put it in perspective; I could see the big picture. Each side, black and white, was in fear, encircled by its own worries and troubles.

I had crossed another borderline when I pretended that I was an attorney. Actually, I had crossed two. For the sake of the movement, I crossed the line between legal and illegal action. But there was another borderline, more enduring and metaphysical. I came to understand that all the players in Bogalusa, black and white, were intimately bound together. We were united in the scheme of violence and political upheaval. We shared coinciding anxieties and expectations. We were all players acting out our roles in a corner of humanity. A god observing from the clouds would not see a true borderline between the black and white camps in Bogalusa.

FOURTEEN

Sobol v Perez

On February 20, 1967, we received word that the Supreme Court of Louisiana had denied Richard Sobol's appeal on Gary Duncan's right to a jury trial. Richard called Judge Leon and asked for an appointment to arrange for Gary's bond to be continued while Richard pursued his appeal to the United States Supreme Court. The judge's secretary told Richard that Judge Leon would be available that morning. Don Juneau and I were elsewhere. So Richard drove down to Plaquemines Parish alone.

After Richard's call, Judge Leon told the assistant district attorney, Daryl W. Bubrig, that Richard was coming to the courthouse. Bubrig telephoned Leander Perez Jr., the district attorney. Perez signed the necessary papers to charge Richard Sobol with practicing law without a Louisiana license. Judge Leon then issued a bench warrant for Richard's arrest. Of course Richard had no inkling that he was walking into a trap. No one in Plaquemines Parish had said one word to him about the fact that he was licensed only in New York and Washington, D.C., and yet was representing clients in Louisiana.

Later, Richard learned that Perez Jr. had investigated him at some earlier time. In the inquiry, Perez discovered that Richard and his family had arrived in Louisiana on August 2, 1966, that they lived in a rented apartment in New Orleans, and that they had been paying utility bills, including gas and electricity. Perez also confirmed with the Louisiana State Bar Association that Richard was not a member of the bar. Perez used this information to assert that the law of comity allowing out-of-state attorneys to represent in-state clients only applied to true "visiting attorneys," those temporarily in the area, and not to those who technically resided in the state. Since Richard and his family had been living in New Orleans for more than six months, Perez insisted that Richard was not a visiting attorney but a resident of the state.

When Richard reached the Plaquemines Parish courthouse, he went to meet with Judge Leon. Leon set a new bond for Gary Duncan, at $1,500, pending appeal to the U.S. Supreme Court. After Richard left the judge's chambers, he walked to a public phone, intending to call the LCDC office in New Orleans. While still in the courthouse, and before he could make the call, he was arrested.

Richard was delivered to the Plaquemines Parish prison, finger-printed, and photographed. His belt and tie were removed, and his brief-case, containing all the Duncan case papers, was taken from him. Bail was set at $1,500. A federal court later found the arrest of Richard Sobol so "unusual" that they commented on it in their opinion: "remanding [Sobol] to jail, removing his personal effects, photographing him and setting bail without having to appear before the judge are so out of keeping with what would normally be done to a person of Sobol's professional status that they can only be interpreted as harassment."[1] According to attorneys who testified in the case, the statute had never before been invoked against a visiting attorney.

Richard spent four miserable hours in a twelve-by-fifteen cell with two other white men (presumably there was a separate cell for black prisoners). While in the jail, Richard explained to one of the other inmates that he had been arrested for practicing law without a license, omitting the fact that he handled civil rights cases. This prompted the other prisoner to tell a story he knew about an out-of-state lawyer in Alabama who had also been arrested for the unauthorized practice of law—but that lawyer had represented "civil rights agitators." Richard told me, "I let him believe that I shared his horror over such a 'crime.'" The other lawyer turned out to be Don Jelinek. Jelinek, another New York lawyer, was in charge of the LCDC office in Selma, Alabama. He too had been harassed by the local white community for representing civil rights cases.

Richard demanded that he be allowed to make his one phone call. He called his wife, who was in the LCDC office. Fortunately, she quickly found LCDC's Louisiana-licensed attorney, Don Juneau. Wearing his rumpled gray suit—fitting attire for a backwoods bayou courthouse—Don immediately contacted a New Orleans bail bondsman to drive with him to Plaquemines Parish.

As Don tells it, on the way to Pointe-à-la-Hache, the bondsman kept asking how much money Richard had in the bank and whether Richard owned any stocks, bonds, or real estate in New Orleans. Don assured the bondsman that he had nothing to worry about, that Richard's mother owned property on Central Park West in New York City. The bondsman seemed satisfied.

During the drive, Don's emotions fluctuated between fear for Richard's well-being and amusement over the cosmic humor of it all. I can still picture the first time Don told me the story, several days after the arrest. Don's large body shook with laughter as he recalled how "that boy" Richard Sobol, from the urban sophistication of New York and Washington, was locked in a tiny, dark, and sweltering, segregated cell in the antediluvian bayous. A truly existential experience!

Don Juneau had only disdain for the Southern racists he encountered so often. But he had the advantage over Richard not only in being a member of the state bar but also in knowing his opponents. He understood what racist Southerners were about. He could talk to them in ways that Richard and I could not. Because he knew the culture so well, and perhaps because he could speak their language, officers of the court might mistakenly assume that he was one of them. Judge Leon did not make that assumption.

When Don arrived at the courthouse, he found Judge Leon in the record room leafing through a book and talking with one of the deputy clerks. As Don entered the room, Leon raised his head. Seeing a large, unfamiliar person moving determinedly toward him, he flinched as if he were about to ward off a blow and asked, "You lookin' for me?" When Don indicated that he was there to bail Richard out, Leon directed Don to the sheriff's office, allowing that the judge had nothing to do with bail-bond issues.

After Richard was released, Don and Richard drove back to New Orleans in the rust-brown LCDC Plymouth that Richard had driven down to Plaquemines Parish, leaving the bail bondsman to return alone in his own car. But before Don and Richard left the parking lot, they bent their heads and checked under the Plymouth's body for any signs of a bomb—even though, as each of them admitted to me, they had no clue what a bomb might look like. For their route home, they chose the highway along the eastern bank of the Mississippi, not willing to risk waiting for the ferry.

Several days later, Richard, along with Alvin Bronstein, chief counsel for LCDC, who was based in Jackson, Mississippi, filed a brief in federal district court in New Orleans. They sought to enjoin the officials in Plaquemines Parish from taking any further action that would deny Richard the right to represent Gary Duncan or any other civil rights workers in Plaquemines Parish. The officials to be enjoined included Leander Perez Jr., the district attorney for the parish; Eugene Leon, the parish judge; and Leander Perez Sr. In their brief, Sobol and Bronstein argued that Richard's arrest was nothing other than harassment designed to create a "chilling effect" on civil rights attorneys and on civil rights workers who needed to retain supportive legal counsel. The argument was premised on the widely accepted perception that, given the vengeful racist atmosphere prevalent in the parish, along with the well-known threats and rhetoric of Leander Perez Sr., no local attorney would dare handle civil rights cases there. Thus an outsider like Richard Sobol was essential if African Americans were to receive proper representation.

Richard also believed that the local officials never would have arrested

him if had he been working on, say, an oil and gas case on behalf of
Leander Perez Sr., regardless of whether he was a member of the Lou-
isiana bar or how long he had resided in the state. Richard and Alvin
Bronstein listed Leander Perez Sr. as the first defendant in their brief.
As Perez himself asserted, he was the most powerful person in the parish.
Months later, when Bronstein took Perez's deposition for the trial,
Bronstein asked Perez, "Would you say that you are the most important
leader in the Parish?" Perez did not hesitate in answering, "I would say
that. . . .There is no doubt about it."[2] Richard believed that no one, not
even Leander Perez Jr., would have taken any significant action in the
parish without the elder Perez's approval.*

By listing Perez Sr. first, Richard also obtained the publicity he
sought. Perez Sr. was news in Louisiana. And the more prominent the
case, the more the public would learn about how civil rights attorneys
were frustrated in their efforts to assist blacks and civil rights workers.

Richard Sobol and Alvin Bronstein also wanted the federal government to intervene on Richard's behalf. They believed that if sufficient
publicity attended the case, the U.S. Justice Department would feel the
pressure and be compelled to join the lawsuit. And they were right. In
September 1967, the Justice Department petitioned the federal court
for permission to participate in the case on behalf of Richard. The government was concerned about the harassment of blacks and civil rights
workers in Louisiana and other Southern states and wanted to guarantee
that African Americans in the South would receive adequate legal representation. In deference to the federal government, the court permitted
the Justice Department to intervene.

In August, before the Justice Department officially joined the case,
Alvin Bronstein, as chief counsel for LCDC, drove down to New Or-
leans from his office in Jackson to represent Richard in his lawsuit.
Richard Sobol and Alvin Bronstein had obtained a preliminary injunc-

---

*Perez Sr. was known to everyone in the parish and to his supporters elsewhere
as "Judge."

tion in federal court enjoining the prosecution of Richard. But they were now seeking a permanent injunction and a declaration that the Louisiana statutes regulating the practice of law were unconstitutional as applied to out-of-state lawyers in general and to Richard Sobol in particular. They received help from Tony Amsterdam, the University of Pennsylvania civil rights expert.

On August 11, in the Maritime Building in New Orleans, Bronstein took Leander Perez Sr.'s deposition. I was not there. The day before, about twenty blacks from Bogalusa had begun a ten-day march through heavily Klan-populated parishes to Baton Rouge, and I had joined them. But I heard all about the deposition. If the underlying issue had not been so serious—in that Richard could be imprisoned if he lost—Perez's deposition would have been entertaining. It was certainly absurd.[3]

When Bronstein introduced himself and Sobol to the short and sturdy Perez, Perez said, "Would you write that on a piece of paper? I'd like to see the names written out, because Soboloff and Bronstein, it sounds like Russian to me." I wondered if this was Perez's oblique way of expressing anti-Semitism. Later, responding to a question about out-of-state lawyers representing clients in Plaquemines Parish, Perez said, "So, if you are a member, for instance, of the American Civil Liberties League [Union] or of any other Communist organization . . . we would make it very inconvenient for you in the Parish of Plaquemines. We don't welcome that kind of trash, or rats and law violators who would destroy our system of government."

Referring to Richard Sobol's practicing out of state, Perez declared, "[I]f I saw him agitating unthinking Negroes to disturb the peace, I'd handle him personally, as a man. Yes, I'd stop him, and try it and see, Mr. Sobol. We pride ourselves in being real Americans, red-blooded Americans with courage enough to defend ourselves and to protect ourselves against those who would set up unlawful demonstrations leading to violence. Try it and see." Pursuing this challenge to Richard, Perez asserted, "We will protect the peace and good order of our community. And we fortunately haven't had anybody to try and disturb it yet. Now, if you want to try your luck, Mr. Sobol, if that's the type of a character you are, you try it."

"I'm Mr. Bronstein," Alvin Bronstein replied.

"I don't know. You look like Sobol. Who is Sobol?"

When Bronstein asked Perez about whether CORE's presence in the parish would constitute a breach of the peace, Perez remarked, "When I first saw a letterhead from Core I sent it to Washington, to check the membership of their directors. And about three fourths of them belonged to—are members of various Communist front organizations."

Bronstein also quizzed Perez about Fort St. Philip and whether it was truly designed to imprison civil rights workers. Perez confirmed that it was. "Yes, of course, because we felt that our jails were not large enough to accommodate the large numbers of demonstrators, disturbers of the peace and law violators that visited other areas. So, we prepared for them." And, correcting Bronstein's use of the term "civil rights workers," Perez added, "Civil rights workers are strictly a misnomer, and a cover up for Communist's [*sic*] activities in this country." Moreover, Perez claimed, "Civil Rights workers, in my books, are simply tools of communists agitators in this country, and they're the demonstrators, of course, which go hand in hand with the Communist conspiracy which strive for national disunity, and they have succeeded beyond their fondest dreams to extend an armed rebellion and destruction of billions of dollars of property with Molotov bombs and shooting of police and firemen in the back, and all this is agitated and sponsored by the Communists who organize these various, so called Civil Rights demonstrations."

To further expose Perez's belligerence toward the civil rights movement, Bronstein urged Perez to admit that he had once said, "[I]f Martin Luther King comes in, we'll guarantee his transportation across the river—part way, that is." Perez did not deny that he had made the statement, adding that it "depended on his conduct." Then Perez testily snapped, "Hey are you defending Martin Luther King? Is he one of your idols?"

Perez had no reservations about revealing his attitude toward African Americans. "I know that Negroes, generally, are immoral. I know that a large number or a large percentage of Negroes have illegitimate children, attest to that fact. There's no doubt about that. I might add that I'm not anti-Negro. I'm anti-Communist, and I'm against the Communists using the Negroes for their purposes. And that's proven all over the country."

"Do you believe that the Negroes have equal intelligence as a rule with white people?" Bronstein persisted. Perez promptly answered, "Of course not." He admitted that there were "a few exceptions," but he agreed with the statement that "generally, Negroes, including Negro lawyers, would not be as intelligent or competent as white lawyers."

Perez had to interject his thoughts on the "Communist-Zionist conspiracy" too. In response to a question as to whether the Civil Rights Act was a Communist conspiracy, Perez said, "That is correct, no doubt about that. Of course it is. I read a Zionist book report—well, a few years ago. It was a secret book report. . . . And integration is a part of the Communist conspiracy, Communist-Zionist conspiracy. The record proves that."

Bronstein questioned Perez about a statement that Perez had made before the House Judiciary Subcommittee in connection with civil rights legislation. "Now, I know that the action of certain hooded men in Mississippi, recently, is decried and condemned. On the other hand, let us realize what the situation is. There have been rapes in the South, and the law has been allowed to follow its course and the cases have come up to the United States Supreme Court and with very few exceptions, if any, the United States Supreme Court has set free the rapists. So, what is the attitude of the Southern gentleman to protect his wife and daughter?" Acknowledging that the quote was accurate, Perez explained, "[T]he Ku Klux Klan was originated by Southern gentlemen of the highest character, professional men, former military men and so forth, to protect the white womanhood against Negro rapists."

At the close of the session, Bronstein thanked Perez for coming. Indignantly, Perez spewed, "Don't thank me, I'm not thanking you."

"Your manners, sir, are no concern of mine," rejoined Bronstein.

"What?" objected Perez. After Bronstein repeated himself, Perez said, "You're not questioning my manners, are you? Don't get personal. Are you?"

Perez's lawyer intervened. "Judge, he's not questioning your manners. He knows better than that."

"I guess he does," breathed Perez. "That's one thing I demand, is respect."

"Respect given where respect is received is a general rule," Bronstein tossed out as he ended the session.

FIFTEEN

"Throw Me Something, Mister"

I had planned to return to New York sometime in February, but with Mardi Gras fast approaching I decided to extend my stay. Law school would wait. I had seen wildly decorated floats winding through the French Quarter for weeks before the big day, and I had heard about the dancing and riotous parties in the streets. It was all about good times and cheer, I was told. But good times and cheer were the last things I uncovered during the days leading up to Mardi Gras. Perhaps because of my awareness of civil rights issues, all I could see were racism and white caricatures of black culture, and all I could feel were abhorrence and fear.

Fat Tuesday, Mardi Gras, precedes Ash Wednesday: in Catholic tradition it offers one last celebration before the rigors and fasting of Lent. The period leading up to Mardi Gras, called Carnival, begins on the Feast of Epiphany, the twelfth night after Christmas. Mardi Gras as New Orleans knows it began in 1857, before the Civil War, when the "Mistick Krewe of Comus" paraded through the city. A krewe, or carnival club, is an aristocratic family's secret society. Most of the major krewes take their names from Roman, Greek, and Egyptian mythology. During Carnival, more than sixty krewes hold private masked balls and parties while they prepare for their elaborate parades.

For weeks prior to Mardi Gras, New Orleans dressed up. Every day another krewe paraded its float through the French Quarter. There was a hierarchy among the krewes, and the more prestigious the krewe, the closer their parade to Mardi Gras day. Until 1992, Comus, the oldest krewe, always retained the honor of parading on Mardi Gras itself, as a kind of grand finale. But in 1992, New Orleans adopted an ordinance banning discrimination in Mardi Gras organizations. Rather than open its secret society to women, blacks, Jews, Italians, or working-class whites, Comus leaders (whose identity was "secret") canceled the krewe's appearance at Mardi Gras. Two other upper-crust, old-money krewes, Momus and Proteus, also canceled their parades.

The most distinguished krewes were expected to provide the most lavish displays. The floats of the old-money krewes were built from wood, cloth, and papier-mâché, and each usually illustrated a theme. Krewes spent nearly the entire year preparing for Carnival. When completed, the floats, often twenty-five to thirty-five feet long and sixteen to eighteen feet high, were towed by trucks and tractors through the streets. Today, with the disappearance of several of the old-money krewes, the city has compensated by creating commercially oriented krewes, whose floats are five to ten times larger.

In February 1967 I watched the krewe members sitting high on the floats, in elaborate and often garish costumes and masks, and waving to the crowds as they drove by. They threw down richly colored necklaces and bracelets and doubloons—gold- and silver-tinted coins bearing pictures and inscriptions of the krewe. Sometimes they also tossed nickels and pennies to the kids. While people gathered along the streets to watch the floats ride by, children, and not a few adults, ran up to the floats screaming for the riders to throw them trinkets. It seemed like harmless fun.

Harmless, that is, until the evening I stood at the corner of Esplanade and Decatur, near the French Market. I was watching a float roll by while some black children called out for trinkets. "Throw me something, mister, throw me something, mister," they chimed as they ran by

A black man exiting through a "White Men Only"
door in the county courthouse, Clinton, Louisiana, 1964.
© Bob Adelman, Magnum Photos, Inc.

Lining up to register to vote, Clinton, Louisiana, 1964.
© Bob Adelman, Magnum Photos, Inc.

A woman registering to vote in Baton Rouge, Louisiana, 1964.
© Bob Adelman, Magnum Photos, Inc.

Funeral of Deputy Sheriff O'Neal Moore, one of the first two black deputy sheriffs hired by Washington Parish, who was killed in an ambush. Left, Robert Hicks (a Mason) is carrying the casket. Note the white government agent in sunglasses on right. June 1965. Courtesy AP/Wide World Photos.

Robert Hicks, 1967. Courtesy Barbara Sobol.

From left: Richard Sobol, Don Juneau, and Gayle Jenkins, 1967. Courtesy Barbara Sobol.

From left: Peter Jan Honigsberg, Robert Hicks, Gayle Jenkins, and A. Z. Young, 1967. Courtesy Don Juneau.

Lolis Elie, partner in the activist law firm of Collins, Douglas, and Elie, 1997. Photo by the author.

Gary Duncan, the petitioner in Duncan v Louisiana, *the United States Supreme Court case that established the right to jury trials in criminal cases in all fifty states, 1967. Courtesy Georgia Guillot.*

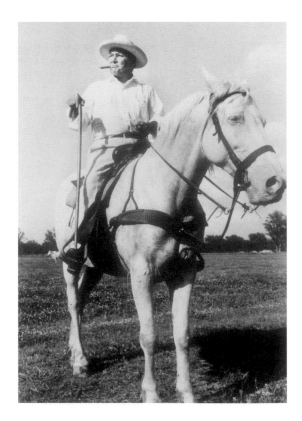

Leander Perez Sr. Courtesy The Louisiana Collection, State Library of Louisiana, Baton Rouge, Louisiana.

State troopers and National Guardsmen walking alongside Bogalusa marchers through Ku Klux Klan territory at Denham Springs on the way to Baton Rouge, August 1967. Courtesy AP/Wide World Photos.

A. Z. Young addressing the crowd at the state capitol at the end of the ten-day march from Bogalusa to Baton Rouge, August 1967. Courtesy the Advocate, Baton Rouge, Louisiana.

Robert Hicks, 1997. Photo by the author.

Gayle Jenkins, 1997. Photo by the author.

me. Two men on the float spotted the black kids, and, after looking around, realized that there were no longer any white kids reaching out their hands. Rather than toss the trinkets to the black kids, the men hurled the heaviest necklaces and coins directly at the black kids' heads. To me, it was an act ripe with malice. Fortunately, the men were so drunk that they missed, and the kids, oblivious to the hostility behind the masks, raced to retrieve their booty.

The more parades I watched, the more apparent it became that the people on the floats were always drunk, no matter what the time of day. Under the circumstances, a little liquor went a long way. The masks, often made of heavy cloth and even leather, covered the wearers' noses and sometimes also their mouths, intensifying the effect of the alcohol as the revelers inhaled the fumes. Even the drivers indulged, and the floats would sometimes lurch off course. There was usually a toilet in the middle of the float, tented by a large sheet, but few riders bothered to use it, and drunks who got up to try often thought better of it and quickly sat back down.

There was a minor scandal that year. People who caught the beaded necklaces and bracelets were outraged to find that they were made in Czechoslovakia. The *Times Picayune* newspaper and the local television news shows had a heyday trumpeting that the patriotic New Orleans elite had purchased trinkets from a Communist regime. Most people failed to see the irony or humor in this.

Observing the mean-spirited revelers fling coins at the black kids was only the beginning of my initiation into Mardi Gras. As I waited on Chartres Street one evening for a float to roll by, I saw a dozen or so black youths carrying flaming gasoline torches. Wearing handkerchiefs on their heads and white sheets on their bodies, they were dancing and gyrating around the float as it wove its way through the streets. I learned that they were known as "Flambeaux."

Flambeaux was the French word for the gas torches used to light the path of the parade. But it was also used to describe the black figures careening around the street and between the floats. People cheered them on, but I was horrified. The ritual seemed to me a deliberate and demeaning parody of black people. I had once heard that black Uncle Toms were disparagingly referred to as "handkerchief heads." In the 1940s and 1950s, black men who wore handkerchiefs on their heads to preserve their conks, or processed hairdos, were also sometimes called "handkerchief heads." Were the Flambeaux caricaturing their own culture? Or, more likely, did the local white society include the Flambeaux to serve as a contrast to the opulently costumed, "dignified and noble gentlemen" above them on the floats? I left. I had seen enough for that day.

Later that week, when I inquired about the Flambeaux, a local friend told me a rumor. In 1964 and 1965, the parade organizers could not encourage a large enough group of blacks to participate. So the white organizers recruited blacks from the local jail, releasing them for the day in exchange for performing as Flambeaux.

By the winter of 1967, the civil rights movement had made impressive gains. True equality was still a long way off, but at least the country had recognized the need for equal treatment and equal opportunity for African Americans. Black people were taking a new sense of pride in their identity and their accomplishments, and white society was recognizing the need to change its stereotypical image of the black race. Yet in New Orleans at Mardi Gras no one seemed to notice the incongruity of these caricatures.

Even more disturbing, the role of the Flambeaux was one of only three options for blacks who wanted to participate in the Mardi Gras festivities. The other two choices seemed to me, an outsider, equally dubious representations of African American culture. One was to belong to the one black krewe, known as the Zulu Social Aid and Pleasure Club; the other was to dance and parade in an "Indian" krewe (in which black people dressed as American Indians). Except for the Zulu and Indian krewes, krewes in 1967 were entirely white and ethnically pure, excluding Italians and Jews—and working-class whites.

The Zulu krewe was formed in 1909 with the expressed intent of mocking the elite and segregated white krewes. And the Zulu krewe lived up to its name. The blacks on the floats, wearing blackface, wore "African-looking" wigs, white gloves, and grass skirts. They carried spears and coconuts, which they tossed off the float to onlookers. Occasionally they featured witch-doctor and snake-charmer themes.

Watching the Zulu krewe dance wildly on its float, I did not believe it was conceived to mock white carnival clubs. Instead, I guessed, the blacks who had started the krewe created the outlandish Zulu image to mock their own people and thus make their krewe acceptable to the white culture. Unless the blacks mocked themselves, they would not be allowed to participate. A more sophisticated, classy Carnival parade and float, such as one depicting a history of jazz, would not be tolerated. The Zulu krewe creation was consistent with the Minstrel, Step'n'Fetchit, and Little Black Sambo images of black people that endured in the white patrician community.

Behind the Indian krewes lay more complex cultural interplays. For over one hundred years, African Americans have dressed in elaborately beaded, feathered costumes and headdresses to become Mardi Gras Indians. During Mardi Gras, they would chant, dance, and parade through the black neighborhoods, often competing to see who was the "prettiest." Each "tribe" or krewe represented a neighborhood, and each neighborhood took great pride in its tribe's costumes and performance. The Indian tribes honored African and Afro-Caribbean heritage and culture in their call-and-response chants and in the rhythms of the music. The most famous tribes were, and still are, the Wild Tchoupitoulas—the Neville Brothers record some of their music under the Wild Tchoupitoulas name—and the Wild Magnolias.

The relationship of blacks and Native Americans may trace its roots to the times when slaves who escaped from plantations found sanctuary in Indian villages. But the Mardi Gras Indian motif was decidedly a black tradition. And it seemed to me in 1967 that no matter how proud African Americans were of their Mardi Gras Indians, or of the fact that much of the music of Carnival was created by black artists, those who wanted to participate in Mardi Gras could not join in on their own terms but only as caricature Flambeaux, Zulus, or Indians.

The Zulu krewe still participates today, but now they use gold-painted plastic coconuts that appear to be among the most prized "throws." In the early 1990s the Zulu Social Aid and Pleasure Club was accused of discrimination for refusing to allow women into the club. When the Mardi Gras antidiscrimination ordinance was passed in 1992, leaders of the club announced that if they were forced to accept women, they might discontinue their parades. The Zulu club has had no problems with race, though. White men have participated for years.

On Mardi Gras in 1967, everything in New Orleans closed down except for the bars. No government or private business offices were open; no mail was delivered; many streets, especially in the French Quarter, were blocked off. In the Quarter, crowds packed the sidewalks. People spilled their drinks over themselves and others, pressed against and swaying along with the other sweating, drunken bodies, their voices cheering and howling.

I tried to walk down Decatur Street early in the morning, when the crowds were less massive than they would become, and passed several drunken men in their twenties with six-packs hooked onto their belts. As I passed the man closest to me, he swung out his arm and punched me in the jaw. The other drunks, his companions, laughed and stumbled on. I was in a town not my own. I too walked on.

In the late afternoon, when the energy of the crowds had become scary, I waded through the drunks, the spilled beer, and the vomit, down to an address on Chartres Street. There, in one of the apartments overlooking the Quarter, I joined friends from the New Orleans "liberal" community in our own celebration. Several were graduate students at Tulane. Because they lived in a conservative Southern community, this integrated group of friends came to depend on each other in a way that those of us who lived in more open societies did not. In New York City, where many people shared my views and values, I felt no strong need to bond with any one of them. So my friendships in New York lacked the intensity and closeness of this singular group in New Orleans. I envied them.

On Mardi Gras, they had all gathered to share a big pot of seafood gumbo and drink beer and wine. After my unsettling experiences on the streets, I was anxious to get inside and join the party. As Bill opened the door to his home, I could see the others sitting cross-legged on the floor, bowls of gumbo and shrimp shells scattered here and there, all smiling broadly. Someone reached out to offer me a joint. Actually, it wasn't quite the typical joint. Instead, they introduced me to a new way of smoking marijuana—inserting the joint into a hole punched into the top of a toilet paper roll and inhaling through the end of the roll. The high would be higher, they claimed. Whatever. I just wanted to chill out with friends.

Someone spoiled the moment by reminding us that we could be sentenced to twenty years in state prison for smoking weed. Louisiana, like most of the Southern states, had harsh penalties for possession of even small amounts of marijuana. Knowing we were hardly considered pillars of the local community, several of us soon got paranoid. It took me a while to relax again by reminding myself that the police were no doubt out there enjoying the day themselves, probably also imbibing. And given the massive, inebriated crowds, there would be more than enough trouble down on the streets to keep them busy. They would not need to look for felons in the flats above. But we kept our windows closed anyway.

The next morning, as the sun shone brightly over the littered French Quarter streets, I made my way around the crushed Jax and Dixie beer cans and broken bottles, intent on reaching the Café Du Monde. The line was long, but it moved fast. I ordered my usual three beignets and carton of chocolate milk, packed them up, and hailed a taxi to the airport. In a few hours I was back in the cold, dreary, but open community of New York.

SIXTEEN

Unsettling Experiences

Spring and summer 1967 were heady times, intellectually and emotionally. Drama, discord, and passion were in the air. A monumental change in the movement was on the horizon. Every day mattered.

During spring semester at New York University I fervently researched the law on jury trials for the *Duncan v Louisiana* case, which was on its way to the Supreme Court. Classes were in session, but my attendance was sporadic. Not only was I thrilled by the idea of working on a constitutionally historic case, but I felt compelled to do the best I possibly could. If we were to win, I believed all our work, including my research, had to be flawless. An error could be disastrous both for Gary Duncan's case and for my own reputation. Besides, Richard Sobol was placing his trust in me (although he didn't have a lot of choice, since no other law student had worked for him that winter).

School was out in mid-May, and I caught the next plane south. My first stop, as in the previous summer, was in Jackson, Mississippi. Once again, I had to attend the LSCRRC summer orientation. This time, the keynote speaker was H. Rap Brown, the chair of the Student Nonviolent Coordinating Committee (SNCC).

Much had happened in the movement in the past year, and Rap Brown represented that change. On June 16, 1966, Stokely Carmichael, then the chair of SNCC, had essentially coined the term "Black Power" when he addressed a rally of marchers in Greenwood, Mississippi. The marchers were volunteering to walk in the place of James Meredith, who had been shot several days earlier on his solo "Walk against Fear" from Memphis to Jackson. Carmichael had taken his cue for Black Power from the writings and speeches of Malcolm X, whose autobiography was to me the most inspirational book of the decade.

Black Power reflected a growing militancy in the movement. It was promoted by SNCC and CORE and lamented by the older civil rights organizations, especially the National Association for the Advancement of Colored People (NAACP) and the National Urban League. The NAACP and the Urban League believed that without the white race's full participation, the black race would never gain the respect and dignity it was due. Martin Luther King Jr. tried to find a middle ground in his salt-and-pepper community by advocating "militant nonviolence."

The media leaped on the changes and reported that the rise of Black Power had caused a huge rift among civil rights organizations. No one could agree on the precise meaning of the term: leaders and followers voiced such clarifications as "black supremacy," "black nationalism," "black unity," "black consciousness," and "black pride." With no clear definition, there was no clear direction. One thing was certain, however: the word "Negro" was soon to be history.

Many of the advocates of Black Power strove for economic and political power, power that was then enjoyed only by middle-class African Americans. The civil rights movement was moving too slowly, the Black Power advocates believed. The Black Power message would reach into the poor communities and the ghettos to all African Americans: You can do it by yourselves. Integration was not working, and whites were not really interested in equality between the races. African Americans had to take the reins to promote their goals. It wasn't that whites were to be excluded, but they now had to join the movement on the blacks' terms.

Following in Carmichael's footsteps, SNCC's Rap Brown advanced the message wherever he went. SNCC was considered by movement people to be the most radical of the civil rights organizations. Later that summer, SNCC would further secure its independence by breaking off from Martin Luther King's integrationist movement and adopting a distinct separatist philosophy. Brown and Carmichael, along with Floyd McKissick, CORE's national director, and Lincoln Lynch, CORE's associate director, virtually reversed the color of the civil rights movement. The year 1967 marked the end of the large white participation in the civil rights movement.

Rap Brown's speech at the LSCRRC orientation was a warning to people like me, white law students. Wearing his not-yet-fashionable tight-Afro hairstyle and shades, he told us that we were no longer here in the South because we wanted to be here. We were here because the Black Power movement granted us permission. The blacks were taking over the movement, and we white people needed to understand that we were to embrace the role of follower.

Not everyone appreciated the significance of his message. Since the movement in Louisiana lagged a year behind Mississippi's, I had not yet felt the influence of Black Power. But by the end of the summer, LCDC students in Louisiana vividly understood the meaning of Rap Brown's words—and it was a very unsettling experience. I spent much of the summer continuing to do research and write memoranda for the *Duncan v Louisiana* and *Sobol v Perez* cases. I was also traveling to Bogalusa again, along with Ruth Robinson, an African American law student from Vanderbilt, and Lisa Molodovsky, a Yale law student. We drove up, sometimes separately, sometimes together, to interview black employees at Crown Zellerbach's paper mill for our employment discrimination case against the company (*Hicks v Crown Zellerbach*).

The boycotts on Columbia Road were still going strong and making an appreciable dent in the local economy. But although we were seeing changes in school integration, employment opportunities, and access to public accommodations—not one cafe refused to serve African Americans by the end of the summer—the fight for equality was not over.

Racism was now expressed in more subtle forms. The better jobs were still not available to the black community, and whites were deliberating whether to abandon the public schools and establish their own private schools. Thus, to keep the Bogalusa movement in the public eye, the leaders of the black community decided to hold two marches that summer. One was to Franklinton, the capital of Washington Parish. The other was to Baton Rouge, the state capital. The second march, which came at the end of the summer, led to a major confrontation between the blacks of Bogalusa and the southern Louisiana Klan.

One of the law students who worked for LCDC with me that summer was Michael Millemann. He had just completed his first year at the University of Oregon. Since he was not attending an "elite" (read "eastern") law school, he was not given the choice assignments. (The following winter, Michael transferred to Georgetown, a premier law school in Washington, D.C. But in the summer of 1967, people only saw Oregon written all over Michael's face.) Instead he was dispatched to the hinterlands of northern and southern Louisiana, where he was directed to scout racial problems in local communities. Michael still recalls how intoxicating and inspirational that trip was for him.

In one small town Michael met an older woman who was the head of the local SNCC chapter. When Michael called her to arrange a visit, she told him not to meet her downtown but to come to her home. It was too dangerous for both of them if they were seen together in public, she said. As Michael entered her house, the thing that struck him most was not the layout of any room, or even the furnishings, but rather the piles of mattresses heaped up high against all the downstairs windows. It seemed as if he had entered a bunker. As they sat in this citadel, the woman told Michael that integration of the schools was still a long way off and that the local white community leaders were not exactly enamored with her and her chapter. She believed that her two grandsons had been drafted into the army to serve in Vietnam the exact day each turned eighteen because of her movement activity.

In the town of Tallulah, Michael met Zelma Wyche, a fearless black barber who was elected police chief in 1969 and later became mayor. In Minden, Michael helped blacks obtain a small business loan to begin a trucking enterprise. All along the route, Michael met with and gathered information from people involved in integrating parish schools so that LCDC could file actions against school districts that refused to desegregate. These were heroic people, Michael Millemann remembers thirty years later, people who changed his life.

Michael came from a liberal background. His father was a doctor in Oregon who counseled Michael to skip to Canada to avoid the draft. Michael too intended to be a doctor until he flunked organic chemistry at Dartmouth. As he saw it back then, his only other choice was to become a lawyer. He remembers the culture at the University of Oregon Law School as not being all that different from the cold, stuffy, arrogant attitudes and sense of entitlement he encountered at Dartmouth. Both schools were predominantly white and male. Dartmouth did not allow women; Oregon admitted two. In his first-year law school class of 121 students, one was black.

Michael's experience in the South gave him direction and a reason to remain in law school. No longer was law merely a fallback from medicine. The summer of 1967 propelled him into his calling and was the most important formative experience in his career. "I have an uncompromised joy that I did it," he told me recently.

When those of us who took part in the movement look back, we can't help wondering whether we really made a difference. Undeniably, the civil rights movement made a difference. Our collective presence helped raise the nation's consciousness to the brutality of racism and succeeded in eliminating the most blatant and humiliating forms of discrimination. But for Michael and me as civil rights workers, the real differences we made were not to others but to ourselves. Michael and I have both become educators, and our experiences in the South have been instrumental in our formation into adults and as contributors to society.

Michael Millemann believes in the law because of what he saw in

Louisiana. The law directly remedied injustices in voting, employment, and schooling. Law gave Michael the tools he needed to redress wrongs, and his experiences in Louisiana gave him the impetus to pursue them. Today, as a professor at the University of Maryland, in one of the foremost clinical law programs in the country, Michael uses the law to help the local community every day. And to each of his students he imparts his strong conviction that the law can make a difference.

When students look back on their classes, they often think of their teachers rather than of any particular piece of knowledge acquired. Legal educators who experienced the civil rights movement firsthand—and in perusing the *Directory of Law Teachers*, I am amazed at the number of law professors who participated—communicate their history in their beliefs and attitudes in the classroom. I hope they can inspire today's students to carry on the movement for equality in our infinitely more complex world.

Although most of the people in the movement were serious, intense types, there were always a few who seemed out of touch with the reality that civil rights workers faced. And where reckless and foolhardy behavior could cost injuries and even lives, these people put others in danger.

On one trip back to New Orleans from Bogalusa, Michael Millemann and I were joined by another law student, whom I'll call Sam Gold. We stopped at a gas station before crossing the Lake Pontchartrain causeway near Slidell. Perhaps it was because we were in Michael's blue Volkswagen Bug with Oregon plates, or because two of us were dressed in the civil rights "uniform" of blue work shirts and jeans, or because Sam wore granny glasses and had long black hair; whatever the reason, it did not take long for the gas station attendant to figure out that we were neither locals nor tourists.

Instead of walking to the island to pump gas into our car, he strode over to the cash register and pulled out a gun. He waved it over his head but said nothing. I remember thinking, "This man looks deranged," as

I watched his mouth crease into a smirk. What was it about white gas station attendants around there? Were they really more simple-minded than other whites? Perhaps they were among those who had the most to lose if ever the black community succeeded in gaining equal opportunities to employment.

Michael and I exchanged looks and headed for the car, deciding that gas might be less expensive elsewhere. I called to Sam, "We're leaving. Let's go."

But Sam was not ready to leave. He walked up to the attendant and started chatting with him. I couldn't hear exactly what he was saying. It was something along the lines of "What are you going to do with the gun?" and "What kind of gun is it, man?" He also remarked that the gun was "far out."

Sam was honestly trying to "relate." He was a child of the sixties, a "trusting soul"—a wealthy one—who defined any circumstance in which he found himself as "mellow." His reflections usually ended with that inane phrase made famous by Sonny and Cher: "The beat goes on." Sam was one of those people who joined the civil rights movement out of genuine good-heartedness but who lacked common sense in a crisis.

Sam would have persisted in his prattle if Michael had not turned the ignition and driven a few feet. Again, we shouted, "We're leaving. Get in!" He saw we were serious. Perhaps against his mellow judgment, but afraid of being left with no ride home, Sam jumped in. We sped away.

In the car Michael and I let loose. Sam's actions could have gotten us killed. The civil rights movement in the South was more than a far-out notion. People weren't all flower children down here. Maybe someday the world would change, and we would all love each other. As yet, however, peace and love had not reached the service station on the north end of Lake Pontchartrain.

Over time, Sam became more of a liability. People asked Richard Sobol not to send him with them to Bogalusa. Eventually, Sam was left alone to do research, or whatever, by himself. He spent much of the summer tooling around the city in his sports coupe.

On his way back home, heading west with a friend, he got into an accident, damaging the car. Sam abandoned the car on the shoulder of the highway, and they hitched a ride to the airport. I heard from friends that after graduating from law school, Sam joined a religiously inspired cult and had been seen at street corners selling balloons to raise money for the cult. Years later, a friend saw Sam at city hall carrying an over-sized black briefcase. The friend inquired whether Sam was now practicing law. No, Sam replied, he was at city hall because he had become a Fuller Brush Man, and this was a good time of day to catch the clerks and other court personnel. Then he clicked open the bag to display his brushes.

A few days after Michael Millemann and his wife, Betsy, arrived in New Orleans, I invited them to cruise Bourbon Street with me and soak up the ambience. About three blocks into the French Quarter, we heard a band playing ragtime jazz. We crossed the street and entered the club. We hadn't been there ten minutes when the band swung into a rousing rendition of "Dixie." As if on command, everyone in the club stood up. The three of us looked at each other quizzically. Several people nearby must have noticed that we were flustered. They muttered and pointed to us.

I thought of the scene at Rick's bar in *Casablanca* where the Nazis rise to sing their anthem and the rest of the patrons respond with the "Marseillaise." But I was not about to lead a counter-chorus of the civil rights anthem, "We Shall Overcome." It was time to leave. We rose, squeezed by some good ol' boys—who, perhaps because Betsy was with us, moved aside—and exited. Outside the door locals joined in the refrain. It was beginning to look like a real Southern good-timey convention. We quickened our pace, turned the corner, and headed as fast as we could to the safety of the tourist crowds along the Mississippi River.

SEVENTEEN

"We'll Bring Your
Freedom Back to You"

The summer of 1967 saw a change in direction in the Bogalusa civil rights movement that corresponded to similar changes in the movement elsewhere in the South. Black Power was on the rise. Perhaps influenced by the previous two summers of unrest in Watts, Detroit, Newark, and other cities, Southern blacks were becoming more assertive in demanding their rights. In Bogalusa, this new assertiveness took the shape of marches. The march on Baton Rouge made headlines throughout the country. And it was the climax of that march that told me my time in the movement was nearly over. The Black Power chant, "Move on over or we'll move on over YOU!" came home to me. As a white man—civil rights worker or not—I too had to "move on over."

The first Bogalusa march took place on July 23. It was led by A. Z. Young, president of the Bogalusa Voters League, with Robert Hicks and Gayle Jenkins as organizers and parade marshals, and by Lincoln Lynch, associate director of CORE. The leaders announced that they would march from Bogalusa through the long-leaf yellow pine forests and flatlands of southeast Louisiana to the parish courthouse in Franklinton, twenty-five miles away. The League sent telegrams to President Johnson, the Justice Department, and several senators and Congress members, proclaiming that the march was called because of the "intimidation, harassment and terror imposed upon Negroes in exercising their constitutional rights."[1] "Negro" was still the current term in Bogalusa then. It wasn't until Lincoln Lynch's militant orations at the end of this march and at the later march to Baton Rouge that the community exchanged "black" for "Negro."

To keep the movement in the spotlight, Gayle, Bob, and A.Z. set out a list of demands they wanted the Washington Parish government to address. Through our LCDC office, A.Z. Young issued a press release that expressed outrage at the "inferior status [of blacks] under law, [and] the lack of justice for Negroes." The march was intended to demonstrate that "Negroes may safely traverse the highways of this state at night, without fear of violence or intimidation." The march was also to be seen as "an affirmation by the Negro community—an affirmation to continue with increased determination and dedication the struggle for economic, political, social and legal equality—an affirmation to [persevere], despite any violence or intimidation directed against such efforts—and an affirmation that if local or state or even federal authorities fail to provide the requisite protection, the Negro community shall provide it themselves."[2]

In his statement, A.Z. Young itemized several "outrageous incidents" over the past two years that reflected the "double standard of justice" applied by state and local law enforcement authorities when blacks exercised their constitutional rights. He reviewed the major acts of violence against the black community over the past years:

> The brutal attack on the first two Negro deputy sheriffs in the history of Washington Parish [in which one was murdered and the other seriously injured, and for which no one had been prosecuted];
>
> The attempted burning of a Negro church by two white men who, despite being apprehended [carrying gasoline], were acquitted by an all-white jury;

The shooting into a Negro church in which members of the congregation were worshipping [no prosecution brought];

The shooting into the car of the wife of a Negro leader [no prosecution brought];

The attempted murder of a Negro army captain home on leave from Vietnam [no prosecution brought]; and

The acquittal by an all-white jury of [a person prosecuted] for the murder of Negro Clarence Triggs. [Triggs had been shot dead along the highway next to a car that had crashed on the roadway and was owned by a white woman.][3]

Before the march could begin, Richard Sobol and Don Juneau had to resolve a legal problem. A Bogalusa city ordinance had been passed just the day before, directed at the black demonstrators, that prohibited night parades. When a similar ordinance had been adopted two weeks earlier, LCDC had filed a motion in federal court arguing that the ordinance restricted free speech and free association rights guaranteed under the Constitution, and Judge Frederick Heebe in New Orleans had ordered the city of Bogalusa not to enforce it. Now a second ordinance banning night marches was in force. But the marchers did not want to wait. Leaving LCDC no time to sue in federal court to void the second ordinance, the leaders began their march in the afternoon, planning to be outside the city limits by six o'clock.

Approximately 125 blacks, many of them teenagers, began the march. The older marchers wore their customary straw hats with buttons reading "CORE NOW." I didn't expect much action on this march, and in fact little happened, but there were threats of violence. Three hundred whites, mostly teenagers and young adults, gathered at the Dairy Queen on the route. We could not tell how many might be armed. Three white teenagers who were urging the crowd to attack the television crews were immediately arrested. The local police moved the crowd off the highway and into a vacant lot across the street. To our surprise, the whites did not say or do anything as the march passed by. Later, someone hurled at A.Z. Young the body of a dog whose throat had been slashed. The dog wore a placard that read, " Smell like a Nigger, A.Z. Young Next."

At the city limit, approximately fifty Louisiana state troopers, many on horseback, and the Louisiana state police riot squad took over escort duties from the Bogalusa police force. The marchers planned to walk slowly, at around two miles an hour, so as to arrive at the courthouse the next morning at nine o'clock. When they arrived, they walked up the steps of the Franklinton courthouse singing "We Shall Overcome." But when they gathered at the courthouse, the mood rapidly became more militant as CORE's Lincoln Lynch, a forceful advocate of Black Power, stepped up to the platform.

He admonished the crowd, "We are through clapping our hands and marching. From now on, we must be ready to kill." As Lynch saw it, if the "honkies and the rednecks" did not grant the blacks' demands, the blacks would make them; the era of civil rights marches was over, and more direct action was necessary. "I know that many of you have said you are ready to die for your rights. But we can't let that continue to happen. From now on, we must be ready to kill." Taking his cue from militant speeches by H. Rap Brown, Lynch concluded, "If Louisiana starts to burn, it's going to burn, burn, burn." A.Z. Young followed with similar words, promising to "burn up Louisiana" if blacks were not given justice.[4]

According to the *New York Times*, local whites who watched the end of the demonstration did not appear to be disturbed by the mood of the blacks. But the message that Lincoln Lynch gave to the black paraders made its mark on the civil rights workers who were standing there. Though we may not have admitted it even to ourselves, we could see the future collapsing on us too. The civil rights movement in Bogalusa was clearly being pressured to move away from its black-white partnership toward a movement run exclusively by African Americans.

A.Z. Young was probably the Bogalusa leader most susceptible to the militant Black Power rhetoric. He had his ear closest to the ground, and he was the most attuned to the publicity advantages of a more militant stand. Robert Hicks and Gayle Jenkins, perhaps because they were more thoughtful and reflective than A.Z., did not allow the Black Power movement to disrupt their relations with sympathetic and supportive whites. Bob and Gayle understood pragmatically that white lawyers could make the difference for them in the school integration and Crown Zellerbach employment cases. But I think it was more than that. They truly believed there was an equal place for whites in the black struggle. Bob and Gayle had room in their hearts for people of all races.

By the end of the summer, when I joined the second, much longer and more volatile march from Bogalusa to Baton Rouge, the influence of the Black Power movement was becoming very visible outside Bogalusa. It became especially apparent in incendiary Baton Rouge, where many people believed the next inner-city summer riot would erupt.

On August 10, nearly three weeks after the march to Franklinton, the Bogalusa Voters League launched a ten-day march to Baton Rouge, 106 miles away. It intended to present a list of grievances to Governor John J. McKeithen. At LCDC, we were geared up for problems. It would be a substantially longer march, traveling deep into Klan territory along old Highway 190 (190 now parallels Interstate 12), and Klan violence was likely.

Robert Hicks's son Charles, who was attending Southern University in New Orleans, came to join the march. The Louisiana state police snapped a photo of Charles and sent it to his school. On the pretext that Charles had missed too many classes, Southern University, a black college, expelled him.[5]

Rather than file a freedom-of-speech lawsuit over the incident, Robert Hicks called his friend James Farmer, the former national director of CORE. Farmer had visited Bogalusa many times over the years, often chauffeured from the New Orleans airport by Charles Sims, the president of the Deacons, with a pistol on the seat. Farmer had attended the funeral of the murdered deputy sheriff O'Neal Moore in June 1965, and he had visited Bogalusa to lead several other civil rights protests. He arranged for Charles to attend Brandeis University in Boston, on scholarship. Charles enrolled at Brandeis for a year and then transferred to Syracuse University, also on scholarship. At Syracuse, Charles became the first black president of the student body. As Bob says, being expelled from Southern was the "best thing that ever happened to Charles."

Richard Sobol asked me to join the march as a legal "observer." I agreed. But in my heart I knew that I would not merely walk along the sidelines. I understood the importance of the march to the black community, and, once again, I wanted to be there with them.

Across Border Street, I watched the leaders prepare for the march. In addition to the usual barbecue sandwiches and the canteens filled with water, the community was providing a Coca-Cola truck. A member of the Deacons was assigned to drive the truck, and other Deacons were to be posted alongside it. To the state police, the truck appeared to be a source of refreshment and provisions. But beneath all those cases of Coke lay a stockpile of rifles, shotguns, grenades, and carbines. The Deacons never needed to unearth that arsenal, but we all felt safer for it.

When we first set out, Gayle Jenkins waved to a black man standing alongside the road to join us. He shook his head no. "That's okay, we'll bring your freedom back to you," she called.

There was violence all along the parade route. In Holden, on the way to Denham Springs, fifteen white men pushed their way through the police escorts and attacked the black marchers, knocking several down. I noticed that the mounted police looked the other way as the white racists attacked the marchers. I surmised that several of the white state troopers knew beforehand of the attack, or at least pretended not to see it coming. But of course there was no way to prove that any of the troopers were even tacitly involved.

At the end of the day all the marchers boarded trucks that had accompanied us along the route and returned to Albany, a town nearby, to spend the night in black residents' homes. During the night Klansmen burned several crosses in the fields.

The next day the gray sky opened up and the rain fell. The towels and handkerchiefs we had used the day before to wipe away the sweat now served to wipe away the rain. The marchers who had worn their straw hats to block the sun now found they provided protection from the cloudbursts.

We were walking in our sandals, tennis shoes, and boots along U.S. 190, near the town of Satsuma in the Livingston Parish "piney woods." All of a sudden a group of about a dozen whites, who had been hiding in a gravel pit, leaped out and attacked Robert Hicks, A.Z. Young, and other marchers. Several of the attackers were young children, their vengeful expressions even more horrifying than those of the older men. One of the state troopers, who evidently carried out his duties conscientiously and perhaps even admired the charismatic A.Z. Young, yelled, "Watch out A.Z.!" Then the troopers took their positions and pointed their bayonets at the charging whites. But it was too late. The whites had reached Bob and A.Z. and were punching them and knocking them to the ground. The troopers swung their billy clubs and carbine butts at the attackers. A news reporter for Channel 6, WDSU, was attacked with a two-by-four and his camera smashed. At the end of the confrontation, three whites and one trooper were sent to the hospital with head injuries, and eight whites were arrested for disturbing the peace or simple battery.

Watching the troopers did not inspire confidence. If they were forced to shoot, what, I wondered, would stop them from turning their rifles and bayonets on the marchers instead? Anything could happen in a melee, and the state troopers, whose loyalties were probably mixed at best, would never be held responsible.

Not only were the blacks becoming more fearful of violence as each day passed, but rumors started flying that the Klan had planted bombs under a bridge we had to cross to enter the town of Denham Springs the next day. In response to the escalation in violence, the black leaders decided to take the following day off. A.Z. Young, Robert Hicks, and Gayle Jenkins wanted to give the marchers a rest and also give Richard Sobol time to negotiate for more state troopers and National Guardsmen with the Justice Department in Washington and Governor Mc-

Keithen's office in Baton Rouge. Richard, who was still in New Orleans, got to work. He telephoned Hugh Fleischer, an attorney for the Department of Justice, and asked him to send federal troops to protect the marchers. Richard argued that the state police obviously could not do the job. Too many lives were at stake. There was also talk that the state troopers were under orders not to escort the marchers beyond Livingston Parish, the Louisiana parish with Klan activity second only to Bogalusa's Washington Parish.

The Justice Department was not keen on sending in federal troops. The word was that Robert Kennedy, the attorney general, was afraid of setting a precedent of acting too swiftly in state matters. Kennedy was above all a politician. He did not want to alienate local Democratic leaders like the governor or undermine the authority of state law enforcement programs. But some of his subordinates, especially John Doar, the head of the Civil Rights Division, were concerned about the possible havoc if the blacks were not protected. Several times in the past, Doar had appeared in federal court in New Orleans in support of the blacks in Bogalusa. He knew firsthand of the violence committed by the local police and the Klan. Concerns about violence were heightened when Lincoln Lynch, CORE's associate director, announced that if the state authorities did not protect the marchers, the marchers would take matters into their own hands. "The whites all have rifles. . . . Why can't black people carry guns if that's what they must do to protect themselves?"[6] But after talking with Governor McKeithen, who promised to send a sizable contingent of National Guardsmen and additional state troopers to protect the two dozen marchers, the Justice Department agreed with McKeithen that the state could handle the situation.

Richard Sobol and Don Juneau concluded that they too needed to join the marchers as we passed through the potentially incendiary town of Denham Springs. On August 17 Richard and Don wrote their wills, and Richard spent some time in quiet meditation with his wife and two-year-old son. The next day, Don informed me that in his will he had left me all his beloved philosophy books. I was touched. But at the same

time, I thought, "Much good that will do," since Don and I were marching together.

The next morning we all assembled in the camp outside the town of
Walker waiting for the leaders to call us together. It was hot and getting
hotter, with temperatures predicted to rise into the nineties and even
the hundreds. We were all sweating, especially Richard and Don, who
wore sport jackets to distinguish themselves as lawyers. I wore the usual
civil rights attire, blue jeans and a work shirt.

One minute I was scared, the next minute I laughed it off as I registered the numbers of troopers and guardsmen. But I also reminded
myself that my life could be over that day and none of my family or
friends except the few right here would even know. It might be days
before people in New York found out. Still, I refused to call home. Why
frighten them? But the rumors of bombs under bridges would not go
away.

The *New York Times* characterized the march through Livingston
Parish and into Denham Springs as one that "combined the elements
of a civil rights demonstration, a major military exercise, and a first-class
parade for spectators who rarely see one."[7] I did not quite see why we
constituted a "first-class parade," but this was the *Times* talking about
rural Louisiana.

And it was certainly something to see. There we were, approximately
seventy-five blacks—about fifty had come from Bogalusa and from
neighboring towns along the route to join the twenty-five original black
marchers through Denham Springs—and five white lawyers and law
students. The marchers were screened by nearly seven hundred National Guardsmen carrying rifles with fixed bayonets and five hundred
state troopers in full riot gear carrying submachine guns. Governor
McKeithen had announced that none of the guardsmen's guns was
loaded but that the state troopers carried live ammunition. However,
we heard rumors that many of the guardsmen did in fact have bullets.

The blacks walked along the center line of the highway. National
Guardsmen marched three abreast on either side of the marchers, while

the state troopers walked single file along the outside. Four troopers on horseback preceded the marchers. Michael Millemann and I walked at the rear of the march. Behind us were another four mounted state troopers. Richard Sobol, Don Juneau, and Lisa Molodovsky, the Yale law student who had spent much of the summer working on the *Duncan* and *Crown Zellerbach* cases with Richard, walked up front along the side of the highway. A convoy of trucks and jeeps patrolled ahead of and behind the marchers.

Helicopters clattered overhead, the word spreading below that one of them was carrying Governor McKeithen. No doubt frustrated and angry at all the publicity, McKeithen was quoted describing the march as "silly, ridiculous, and absurd."[8]

The town whites were out too, and not exactly passive. While some did no more than gape, others jeered and twisted their faces into mean-spirited expressions, while their eyes remained expressionless. Children sat on their parents' shoulders and waved Confederate flags—maybe they were the ones who evoked the parade atmosphere for the *Times* reporter.

As we marched we saw a group of whites chase some black spectators who had been standing along the route. Fortunately the state troopers saw the incident and rushed in to protect them. A number of onlookers threw eggs and bottles, and several blacks, troopers, and guardsmen (wearing black helmets) were hit. Other whites threw roofing nails and broken glass onto the roadway ahead of the marchers, delaying the march while the soldiers cleared the road. One elderly white woman called out, "Leave the niggers here just five minutes, five minutes, that's all we ask."[9]

Soldiers were positioned at each end of the bridge along the roadway; their purpose was to guard against the planting of any bomb. Dynamite was actually found under one bridge that we were planning to cross. The colonel who headed the National Guard troops announced that the bomb was only a dummy. We did not believe him for a minute. But Don Juneau and I did get a good nervous chuckle out of it later that

evening. After the march had stopped for the day, A.Z. Young compli-
mented the troopers and guardsmen and said that without their protection "there would have been slaughter out here—slaughter."[10]

The next day we walked about five miles to the edge of Baton Rouge.
Governor McKeithen had called out 850 additional National Guardsmen, raising the number to 1,500, but they were not necessary. It rained
most of the day, and any Klansmen who cared to harass us stayed in
their cars. We collected ourselves outside the city in a wooded area. The
rain persisted. We were wet, miserable, and tired.

The Klan held a demonstration outside Baton Rouge that night and
burned a fifteen-foot cross and a Vietcong flag. The black marchers,
joined by local blacks, held their own rally at Capital Junior High
School. It began with people singing civil rights songs, but the tone
soon changed into a more militant one. Lincoln Lynch led the crowd
of approximately four hundred people, many in their teens or early
twenties, in a chant of "Black Power" and "Down with the Honkies."
Referring to some of the worst social unrest in American cities in the
mid-1960s, and very aware of local politicians' fears that police brutality
would lead to similar explosions in Baton Rouge, Lynch declared, "I
mean if it takes a Newark or a Plainfield or a Detroit, then that's how
it has to be. White feet on black necks have been there too long. We've
prayed. We've marched—now the time has come to break the hold."[11]

But the next day, when the marchers and local people from Baton
Rouge held a rally at the Capitol, was the one that Michael Millemann
and I will never forget. H. Rap Brown, the scheduled speaker, had been
arrested the day before for carrying a loaded gun across a state line.
Lincoln Lynch substituted for him and again rallied the crowd with his
talk of Black Power and revolution. "There is no power on earth that
can prevent violence or revolution. The only thing that can be done is
to remove the causes."[12] Much of his speech also focused on the need
for a new movement of Black Power.

Richard Sobol, Don Juneau, Michael Millemann, and I had joined
the crowd at the Capitol to hear the speeches. But soon Michael and I

were separated from Richard and Don, who, we found out later, had decided to return to camp. Although the fury of Black Power laced the speeches, Michael and I tried to act as if the rhetoric was directed at other whites, not at us. After all, we were civil rights workers who supported the concept of "black pride." We belonged. We assured ourselves that the anti-white speeches we were hearing were directed at the local rednecks and Klansmen.

But the mood changed, and it changed fast. Those black faces nearby were not smiling at us anymore—if they ever had been. Maybe, I thought, these were local people who did not know who we were. Whatever the case, Michael and I soon felt ourselves the targets of intense hostility. It felt as if a throng of black youths were signaling each other and moving into position around us.

Michael looked at me in alarm. The realization hit both of us at the same time. We were not in the safe environment we thought we were, and we weren't sure that there was a way out. Suddenly, out of nowhere, a black man, whom I thought I vaguely recognized from Bogalusa, pushed his way over to us. He said nothing but motioned for us to follow him. How he knew we were in trouble, I do not know. I never did get his name. But angels appear to all of us at one time or another, and here was ours. He elbowed his way through the crowd, clearing a path for us and always keeping us in sight. When Michael and I reached the edge of the crowd, he silently disappeared back into the rally. We could hear the rallying cries as we slipped away.

Later that evening, Michael showed his vulnerability, something he rarely did. He spoke of the LSCRRC orientation in Jackson, at which he had arrived feeling hopeful and enthusiastic. But near the end of the orientation, he heard H. Rap Brown's heated remarks on the advent of "Black Power" and his call for black people to distance themselves from "whitey's" laws. He was shocked. For a while it set him back, leading him to question his motivations. However, as he began his summer at LCDC, those thoughts faded. He was inspired by what he saw as he drove through Louisiana, gathering information on civil rights workers, promoting equal rights for blacks in lonely backwater towns. Soon he put Rap Brown's remarks behind him. For the balance of the summer, Michael felt optimistic and positive.

Now, in his last few days before he was to leave the South, Michael was once again subjected to the white-hating, Black Power militancy he had experienced in Jackson. He took it personally; he felt hurt and betrayed. "It seemed like bookends," he later confided to me, "to an otherwise wonderful summer."

In thinking about that incident in Baton Rouge, I find it difficult to sort out my feelings. I did not immediately experience the hurt and confusion that Michael felt. Instead I remember being stunned and numbed by what had happened. In the two years I had been in the movement, I had never considered that the color of my skin would make a difference. I had been oblivious to racial complexities, preferring to see things in simple terms of Us, the integrationists, against Them, the segregationists. But in Baton Rouge, the color of my skin had mattered.

My first reaction was to dismiss the incident as one caused by a group of unthinking blacks who did not know me. What did I care what they thought? The blacks I knew in Bogalusa had always treated me with the highest regard. Indeed, the man who had helped Michael and me at the rally was himself from Bogalusa. I could take comfort in the fact that my skin color would never matter to the people of Bogalusa, and especially not to the two people I had come to know and respect most, Gayle Jenkins and Robert Hicks. If Gayle or Bob had rejected me, my reactions would have been very different; they were people who meant something to me. The threats of the menacing crowd in Baton Rouge were just not the same.

But I also had to accept that not all of the hostility in the crowd came from young punks. It was a large crowd, hundreds of people, who had come to the demonstration with diverse motivations. No doubt there were young African Americans whose beliefs of self-determination for the black community were based on the highest principles. They had come to the concept of Black Power because it made philosophical sense. Then there were the mainstream blacks—many of them middle-aged—people who had been on the march or who had come from the Baton Rouge community. They were sympathetic to white participation in the movement and understood the skills and financial support we could bring. But they also understood that Lincoln Lynch's words needed to be heard. And there were the people on the margin—people perhaps like Charles Sims—who believed in the movement and worked for it, but who also had their own agendas. In the summer of 1967 I could not discern how prominent or powerful the Black Power movement and its message would become among these diverse groups of people. Essentially, I had dismissed the message because of the messenger.

Today I also realize that I had been weaning myself from the civil rights movement toward the end of that summer, and that, too, made it easier for me to distance myself from the events in Baton Rouge. The civil rights movement in Louisiana, as I knew it, was winding down. The twin goals of integration and securing the voting rights for all African Americans had largely been met. I had come to the South to offer my skills and to help light the fire. I had done my part, and no matter how exciting the summer of 1967 had been, it was time for me to move on.

Opposition to the United States presence in Vietnam was heating up. I had been involved in the peace effort for several years, and moving further in its direction was a natural transition. By the time of the events in Baton Rouge, part of me had already taken leave of the South in anticipation of devoting myself to the antiwar movement in New York.

The times had changed, and they had changed forever, for all of us. Yet as sophisticated as we have become over the years, we seem to be no closer to resolving black-white relations. Indeed, the gulf between the races today is in many ways far wider than the line that divided Border Street thirty years ago. The perceptions and suspicions that

African Americans and whites have about each other are borderlines that are harder to cross. We make some progress now and then, but the simple act of crossing Border Street is no more. For me, the summer of 1967 marked the end of the confident and hopeful era of blacks and whites pursuing the goal of equality together.

EIGHTEEN

Moving On

In the fall of 1967, when I returned to law school, anti–Vietnam War activity was heating up. Although many of us in the civil rights movement had opposed the war for some time, we could now dedicate all our energy and passion to antiwar activities. President Lyndon Baines Johnson had intensified the bombing of Vietnam and of neighboring Cambodia while at the same time pulling back from his proclaimed war on poverty. Demonstrators around the country, especially on college campuses, were protesting. Although we never did convince Johnson to end the war, we did succeed in ending his political career when he announced that he would not seek the presidency in 1968.

That fall I participated in a demonstration against Dow Chemical. Dow was the largest manufacturer of napalm, which burned, maimed, and horribly killed Vietnamese civilians as well as troops. Dow was recruiting on the undergraduate campus of New York University. Antiwar leaders invited all NYU students, including those from the law school, to join a sit-in at the recruiting center.

Approximately two hundred protesting students had gathered in the large hallway. We noisily cheered when the Dow applicants, on seeing our protest, turned around and left without interviewing. We chanted the favored antiwar, anti-Johnson refrain, "Hey, hey, LBJ, how many kids did you kill today?" When it became apparent that we would not leave until Dow did, the NYU administration made an announcement. They told us that although they appreciated our concerns, we had made our point and it was now time to move on. In fact, if we did not exit the building within five minutes, we would be treated as trespassers on private property. Any student present after that time would be expelled from the university.

The decision was easy for me. I may have had the most to lose, since I was in my third year of law school, but I was staying. My time in Louisiana had determined that. I had been inspired by watching people in the movement speak out for their beliefs, and I certainly was not going to stop now. Here, sitting in against Dow Chemical, I could step off the sidelines and add my voice to those of others against the war.

The other third-year law students, even those who had worked in the South, all got up to leave. They said that they admired my stance, but that I should save my principles for another time. If I were expelled, I could never become a lawyer and use my legal skills and expertise to help others. Their arguments recalled what Richard Sobol had said to me after I helped integrate the beach at Lake Pontchartrain. But at the time, the most important things to me were being true to myself and doing my part to help end the war. My decision to stay may not have been prudent, but I wanted to be counted on the line.

As they left, two third-year friends said they would support me if any administrative action was taken. All but two of the second-year law students also left. Five first-year law students stayed. The eight of us joined the remaining students from the other NYU colleges and schools.

About fifteen minutes later, after allowing everyone enough time to clear out, the administration sent in the campus police. None of us resisted as security escorted us out. Before releasing us, they wrote down our names and indicated that they would pass them on to the appropriate school or college.

The next day, on my way to class, the associate dean of the law school stopped me in the hallway. His eyes examined his shoes as he explained the quandary in which the law school administration found itself. The last time the law faculty had had a disciplinary issue, he said, was a decade before, when a male law student followed a female law student into the women's bathroom. The law school had no precedents for this kind of thing. Nevertheless, the administration felt compelled to hold a hearing. I asked him how it would be run. Who would preside? Were we allowed to bring counsel? He didn't know. They would have to make up the rules as they went along.

The hearing was held several weeks later in the law school auditorium. The defendants were seated together at a circular table, and our accusers—the administration—faced us from the podium. The "jury" was composed of the entire faculty, over forty professors. We were not permitted counsel, but we had consulted with two civil liberties lawyers the day before. The eight of us tried to raise the issue of motive in our defense, but the administration refused to consider the reasons for our actions. The issue was clear and simple to them: we disobeyed a direct order from the university administration, and we trespassed on private property when we refused to leave. The law school also denied us the defense of freedom of speech. It said that the university was a private institution, and the First Amendment right to free speech applied only in public access areas and thoroughfares. Academic freedom and freedom of speech might have been taught as precepts in NYU Law School, but when the reality hit the institution, those cherished notions were swept aside for the sake of orderly administrative and business practices.

After the hearing we were asked to leave so that a vote could be taken. We learned later that two faculty members had argued forcefully that no penalty should attach to our behavior. Several other professors held out for expulsion. But finally, they all agreed to a compromise: a letter describing the incident was to be included in our personal files.

Such a letter was not as harmless as it may seem. At the end of our third year of law school, these personal files would be submitted to the state bar's character committee—the committee that determined whether we were "morally fit" for the practice of law. Essentially, the law school was abdicating its responsibility by passing the moral issue on to the next level.

Fearing a backlash from the state bar's character committee, we challenged the penalty. When we announced that we were appealing the punishment, the dean and the faculty called it quits. Even the professors who voted to expel us could not bear to repeat the hearing process. The issue was becoming too divisive and time-consuming. Just like most law professors, who tend to be conflict-averse, they wanted to retreat to the safety of the classroom. So, without much further deliberation, the faculty and administration voted to tear up the letters and void the whole episode.

As I recall this incident of thirty years ago, I am reminded of an encounter I had with one of my professors the day following the Dow protest. I had come into his law class unprepared. As was the custom for unprepared students, I took a seat in the back of the room. It was the practice of the professor—as long as students did not abuse the privilege—to excuse people who sat in the back and not call on them during that period. But as soon as class began the professor called on me. I reminded him that I was sitting in the last row and was unprepared. Anticipating my answer, he asked me why. I explained that I had been involved in yesterday's demonstration. His eyes gazed up at me, then at the class. He said that I had come to law school to learn, not to protest, and that I would be better served if I quit those demonstrations and instead focused on my schoolwork. What kind of lawyer did I want to be anyway? He and I both knew the answer.

Again the professor asked me to discuss the case we were reading. Without responding, but feeling a mixed sense of self-righteousness and anger, I collected my books and notes and walked out of the class. No one said a word. And only one friend, a woman who had also worked in the South, seemed to care. She was the only student who spoke to me about the incident later that day. That was the last time I sat in that class that semester. I used my friend's great set of notes and passed the course anyway.

In the winter of 1968 I flew down to New Orleans. My heart was not in the civil rights movement as it had been. Black Power had something to do with it, but I think my withdrawal was broader in nature. My role was not as vital as it had been: I had done all that I could on the cases Richard Sobol assigned to me, and the demonstrations and marches in Bogalusa were coming to a halt. Although complete integration of the local schools and the Crown Zellerbach plant had to wait several more years, the Bogalusa movement had proved largely successful.

There was relatively little LCDC work for me in the three weeks I was in New Orleans. Richard Sobol was in Washington, formulating his argument to the Supreme Court in *Duncan v Louisiana*. He used his old law firm of Arnold and Porter to help him practice for the oral argument. Don Juneau ran the LCDC office, and much of the time he and I worked together on *Hicks v Crown Zellerbach*, drafting yet another brief on behalf of the black employees. We also worked on several school integration cases in parishes in northern Louisiana. Don loved to tease me whenever I referred to these parishes as "upstate." "Upstate is New York," he would gleefully complain. "In Louisiana it's 'northern.' And you're in the South, boy!"

I chose not to stay for Mardi Gras that winter. Once was enough. And although I have been back to New Orleans more than twenty times since then—several times to the fabulous Jazz and Heritage Festival in late April and early May—never have I had any desire to experience Mardi Gras again.

That year, 1968, was a banner year for Richard Sobol. On May 20 the United States Supreme Court decided in his favor in *Duncan v Louisiana*,[1] agreeing that states could not deny jury trials in serious criminal cases. Although Justice Byron White, the author of the opinion, did not need to decide where the actual line was to be drawn between petty offenses that did not require a jury trial and serious crimes that did, he seemed to regard a penalty of a six-month prison term as the dividing line.

Richard called me from New Orleans when he heard the news. He was ecstatic, and so was everyone else in the office. Richard also sent me a gracious note, thanking me for my assistance on the case and pointing out that the court in its decision had referred to my research both on jury trials in the other forty-nine states and on examples of other serious crimes in Louisiana where a defendant would not be entitled to a jury trial.

After the Supreme Court decision, the Louisiana legislature reduced the maximum sentence for simple battery from two years to six months, so that Gary Duncan again faced a trial without a jury. Richard wanted to bar Duncan's retrial, believing that a new trial was nothing more than continued harassment. He filed an action in federal district court to enjoin any further prosecution. Judge Fred J. Cassibry concurred with Richard's position and issued an injunction permanently enjoining Leander Perez Jr., the district attorney for Plaquemines Parish, from retrying Duncan. Cassibry observed that "whether Duncan slapped or simply touched the white youth on the arm, it [was] clear beyond dispute that any violation that may have occurred was so slight and technical as to be generally reserved for law school hypotheticals rather than criminal prosecutions."[2] The judge emphasized that were it not for the civil rights context of the case, Duncan never would have been punished. Perez appealed. The U.S. Court of Appeals for the Fifth Circuit affirmed Judge Cassibry's decision.[3]

Richard Sobol also succeeded in his personal lawsuit against Plaquemines Parish. On July 22, 1968, a three-judge panel in federal district court in New Orleans permanently enjoined Leander Perez Jr. from prosecuting Richard for practicing law in Louisiana. The judges were convinced that Richard was prosecuted only because he was a civil rights lawyer representing a black man in a case growing out of the desegregation of the Plaquemines Parish school system. The sole purpose of the prosecution was to deter Richard and other movement attorneys from providing legal representation to Gary Duncan and to other defendants in civil rights cases.

In its opinion, the panel noted that although Richard was living in New Orleans, he was temporarily present in the state and had no intention of remaining permanently there. At trial Richard had testified that he had extended his one-year commitment to LCDC only because of his obligations to Gary Duncan and to his own personal litigation, which arose from Duncan's case. By accepting Richard's testimony, the panel was able to bypass the broader issue of whether the Louisiana state statutes that regulated the practice of law were unconstitutional as they were applied to Richard Sobol.

Because the court believed Richard's testimony that he was only temporarily resident in Louisiana, Richard felt that he had to leave the state after the case was resolved. In the fall of 1968, Richard, his wife, son, and new baby packed their bags and moved back to Washington, D.C. Richard continued to manage his active cases in Louisiana, commuting to New Orleans every other week.

Since 1991, Richard has been living outside New Orleans. Years before, he passed the Louisiana bar exam. When I met with him in April 1996, I asked him what I should say he's doing now. "Tell them that I am spending one-half my time shoveling dirt"—his home had flooded—"and one-half the time practicing piano," he said. But that is not entirely true. Just a few weeks before our meeting, Richard was in Bogalusa representing six black police officers who were denied access to weekend law enforcement seminars held out of town, seminars to which the white officers were sent.

Richard has also stayed in touch with Gary Duncan and recently represented Duncan, who still resides in Plaquemines Parish, in a case against Shell Oil. Duncan's fishing boat had split in two when it hit an underwater drilling rig in the Gulf. Still the super-lawyer, Richard obtained a very favorable settlement for Gary Duncan in April 1997.

Don Juneau, LCDC's associate counsel, left in 1968 too. He moved to California to work for California Rural Legal Assistance, representing grape pickers and other agricultural day laborers. Years later, Don returned to his home state and until 1998 was the attorney for the Tunica-Biloxi Indian Tribe of Louisiana.

Robert Hicks, Gayle Jenkins, and A. Z. Young continued to lead the Bogalusa civil rights movement. By 1968 the integration of parks, restaurants, and other public accommodations had been achieved. School integration was becoming a reality. In 1971 Judge Frederick Heebe issued his principal opinion on the Crown Zellerbach case, forcing the company to integrate its workforce fully and requiring the separate black and white unions to merge.

After Richard Sobol left, the LCDC office in New Orleans was run by George Strickler and later by Stanley Halpin, who was there when the office closed down in 1971. The New Orleans office was the last of the three LCDC offices to close. LCDC's objective—to provide a legal ambulance service for local blacks involved in the movement and civil rights workers who toured in the South—had been met. Others could now take over. By the early 1970s, every major city in Louisiana had attorneys, both black and white, who were available and willing to assist black communities.

In the summer of 1968 I graduated from New York University School of Law and took the New York bar exam. The day after the exam, I borrowed two hundred dollars from my sister and boarded a plane for California. I stayed with some friends in San Francisco and then found a ride across the Bay to Berkeley.

AFTERWORD

The day I arrived in Berkeley—August 4, 1968—I knew I had found my home. I had journeyed from New York to California via the civil rights movement, understanding instinctively that it was time for me to move on. I had left my sheltered existence in New York, where I had been a naive, intense, and self-righteous young man. My days as an idealistic civil rights worker also had drawn to a close. I was looking for new ways of seeing the world. I did not want my family and past friends around to remind me of who I had been. California's accepting and welcoming spirit suited my temperament.

I certainly did not accomplish my transformation overnight. My early days in Berkeley were marked by self-discovery more reflective of the "tune in, turn on, drop out" and "free love" mantras than of mature insight. I lived in a commune, or something like one. I let my hair grow long and grew a beard. At night I'd listen to Tom Donahue playing Dylan on the new FM radio band or join others in piling into a Volkswagen Bug to drive to San Francisco to see Janis Joplin or It's a Beautiful Day, perhaps, at the Fillmore or Avalon Ballroom. On other nights we'd ride over to Sam Wo's in Chinatown for noodles. The reading matter of choice was Herman Hesse, Carl Jung, and anything on Eastern mysticism, spirituality, and Tibetan Buddhism.

However, I hadn't abandoned the protest movement. I participated in campus demonstrations against the Vietnam War, my eyes streaming from police tear gas any number of times. In May 1969 I was locked in the Alameda County prison farm at Santa Rita for twenty-four hours, along with hundreds of other protesters, for refusing to disperse at a demonstration at People's Park in Berkeley.

In the process of finding myself, I had come across many kindred spirits here in California. For the first time in my life, I could relax, release some of my intensity. I developed new confidence in who I was. My beliefs were affirmed by people with whom I identified; many others were searching too. If the civil rights movement was the start of my soul journey, California's self-realization movement was the next stop.

Through a connection with Don Juneau, I found my first job in Berkeley with the National Housing and Economic Development Law Project, a federally funded center to assist legal aid attorneys. Working flexible hours, I wrote briefs to the California and federal appeals courts and the California Supreme Court on behalf of tenants. I also coauthored a tenants' rights manual for legal aid organizations to use in counseling clients. By working at the Housing Law Project, I realized that I could continue to use my skills to help others as I had done in the South. And I knew I could support myself without having to become the traditional lawyer I never wanted to be.

After I left the Housing Law Project, I wrote several law books for laypersons. The movement to provide self-help legal books for nonlawyers originated in Berkeley. The concept was, and still is, that if equipped with the right information, people could be empowered to represent themselves. Many people are capable of handling relatively minor cases without lawyers if they are given some direction. I wrote books on the rights of people in debt; the rights to unemployment insurance; how to use a law library and research legal materials; and creating a cooperatively owned business. Writing these books reaffirmed my belief that I could make a difference by using my legal education outside a traditional law practice.

When I started a family, it was time to move on again. I could not rely on the royalties that I was earning from the legal books, or on the income from part-time working at the Swallow, a collectively owned restaurant in the University Art Museum. I needed a real job. So I searched for a job teaching law, and, with much serendipity and good luck, I found one. Eventually I moved into full-time teaching, and today I am a professor at the University of San Francisco School of Law, directing the Legal Writing and Research Program and teaching lawyering skills and public interest law classes. I also teach in programs for minority students at two other law schools in the Bay Area.

Partially out of my interest in exploring race relations, I have taught law-related classes at Berkeley High School and Oakland Street Academy. Berkeley High is a large public school that is racially and culturally very diverse. Oakland Street Academy is a small, alternative public school with mainly African American and Latino students. At both schools I raised with the students any number of legal and societal issues, including the kinds of civil rights issues I dealt with as a young man in the South. In one incident at Berkeley High I was starkly reminded of my experiences in Louisiana. The class was discussing the fact that there were no Barbie dolls representing minority cultures when the students were growing up. Carmina, who had told me earlier in the semester that she tried to stay out of class discussions because they were too upsetting and made her angry, spoke up.

"When I grew up, I had a Barbie doll. I loved my Barbie. But she was white. I never had a chance to choose a Mexican Barbie."

"Why don't you write to Mattel, the company that makes Barbie, and ask them to design a Mexican Barbie?" I suggested.

"No," she replied. "You write it."

"Me, why me? Why should I write the letter?" I questioned, indicating that Barbie dolls were of little importance to me.

"Because you're white, they'll listen to you," she said.[1]

As an educator, I try to instill in all of my students the inspiration that I experienced as a young person. Racial issues are much more complex today than when I was in the movement. It's no longer just black and white but a diversity of nationalities and ethnicities. And instead of building bridges of trust, we sometimes create chasms of suspicion between ourselves and others of another race. When we talk about counseling clients and assisting others, I try to engage my law students in thinking about the larger issues of race and culture in society. A lawyer and a client may see the legal issues very differently if they come from dissimilar cultural backgrounds. A lawyer needs to research and learn about a client's heritage and how the client's ethnicity may affect the client's perspectives as well as the options the client chooses.

Have times really changed since the civil rights days? My three children, as well as the students I teach, live in a world very different from the one in which I grew up. Many stark images of the past—separate water fountains labeled "colored" and "white"; blacks directed to the back doors of restaurants; white-hooded Klansmen openly burning crosses; Southern lynch mobs; African Americans turned away at polling booths; police using night sticks to beat demonstrators at lunch counters; and police dogs attacking marchers—have gone the way of the covered wagon. In large part because of the civil rights movement, African Americans have attained some measure of equality in voting rights, jobs, schools, housing, public accommodations, and access to public office. The black middle class has expanded. Certainly we have not attained the movement's ideals. Horrific racially motivated crimes and blatant discrimination still occur. But there also has been a significant increase in the American people's awareness of race-based crimes and discrimination. No longer can a segment of the population commit its terrorist acts or even boldly discriminate with impunity. And progress happens one step at a time.

The American civil rights movement has also sparked other movements. It was the inspiring and motivating force for the Berkeley Free Speech movement, Black Power, the anti–Vietnam War movement, the United Farm Workers movement, the women's movement, and the gay-lesbian liberation movement. Today's concept of multiculturalism derives in large part from the civil rights movement's spirit of liberation.

In spite of the fact that race has often become a volatile and emotional issue, I remain optimistic. Although it probably will not happen in my lifetime, American culture seems to be approaching a sea change. At the close of the twentieth century, I believe that we are moving toward a genuinely racially mixed society. In fact, in California, where many people are of racially mixed descent, it's becoming considerably more difficult to define a child's race. And as the races continue to mix, we will perhaps become less mindful of our racial differences and instead focus on celebrating our many unique cultural strengths. My dream is that in several generations we will have become so comfortable with our "integrated" multicultural society that the issue of race, which bears down on us so heavily today, will no longer dominate our national consciousness. Our children will carry the process along, and we will continue to evolve.

After completing an earlier draft of this manuscript, I gave it to several friends to read. One of the readers surprised me by asking why I had repeatedly returned to Louisiana to work in the civil rights movement. She pointed out that most of the white students who were involved in civil rights work spent only one summer in the South. My first response was that I wasn't sure. I just did it. But, as we continued to talk, I found myself telling her two stories about my parents.

As I mentioned, my mother and father were Jewish, born and raised in Austria. On Kristallnacht, November 9, 1938, when the Nazis terrorized Jews and wantonly destroyed Jewish homes, shops, and synagogues, a Catholic woman hid my father in her house. Concealing a Jew was a crime. When the Nazis came to this woman's door looking for

Jews, she expressed outrage. How dare they accuse her, or even intimate that she would be harboring a Jew, she charged. They abandoned their search, apologized, and left.

Some time later, my father received a letter from the Nazis summoning him to the local train station for deportation to a concentration camp. He ignored it. He disregarded a second communiqué as well. A third dispatch warned that if he did not appear at the station the following morning, they would come for him. That same day, he and my mother received visas to emigrate to the United States.

My parents received the visas because a married couple in America had signed an affidavit agreeing to support my parents for five years if they could not find work. Such affidavits were required by the United States government before it would issue visas to refugees. The people who had signed the affidavit did not know my parents.

As I recounted these incidents to my friend, I suddenly understood that a part, perhaps even a large part, of my motivation for going down South came from hearing stories when I was very young. Three people took considerable risks to save the lives of complete strangers, my parents. Why did they do it? I had wondered from the first time I heard the stories. What had they been thinking when they acted?

I had not consciously recognized it thirty years ago, but in my heart I must have known that by doing my part in the civil rights movement and upholding its commitment to racial justice, I was saying thanks to the people who had been there for my parents. Today I understand that the continuum from these people to my parents to me impelled me to return to Louisiana again and again. Those stories became part of me, and they shaped my future.

Looking back, I can say assuredly that the civil rights movement made a vital and enduring difference for those of us who participated in it. We were profoundly transformed by the experience. The movement gave our lives new meaning. For a moment in time, blacks and whites worked hand in hand with a common vision. And that vision has stayed with us as we have moved through life with our families, our friends, and people we have met. As a friend said, "It changed you, and you passed it on to others."

Thirty years ago, thinking that we were doing God's work, we crossed Border Streets and borderlines. But, most important, we made a difference in ourselves. We reached for the stars and pulled down our own.

NOTES

1. FROM THE SUBWAY TO MISSISSIPPI

1. See Robert Weisbrot's *Freedom Bound* (New York: W. W. Norton, 1990) for a concise history of the civil rights movement.

2. See John Lewis's *Walking with the Wind* (New York: Simon and Schuster, 1998) and Mary King's *Freedom Song* (New York: William Morrow, 1987) for two evocative autobiographies, the former written by a black man, the latter by a white woman, covering the authors' years in SNCC and the movement.

3. August Meier and Elliott Rudwick, *CORE: A Study in the Civil Rights Movement, 1942–1968* (New York: Oxford University Press, 1973).

4. In Tom Dent's *Southern Journey: A Return to the Civil Rights Movement* (New York: William Morrow, 1997, 370–72), Unita Blackwell reflects on the movement and its enduring effect on her and on society.

5. After he left the South, Henry Aronson went to Vietnam to represent deserters. Jack Greenberg, *Crusaders in the Courts* (New York: Basic Books, 1994), 342.

6. Richard Kluger wrote a fascinating account of Houston and Marshall and their victory in the *Brown* case in *Simple Justice* (New York: Random House/Vintage, 1975).

7. Kluger, *Simple Justice*.

8. Thomas Hilbink, "Filling the Void" (unpublished ms., 1993).

9. Details on LCDC's inception and objectives were contributed by John de J. Pemberton, who was the executive director of the ACLU in 1964; Richard Sobol, the first chief staff counsel for LCDC's New Orleans office; and Stanley Halpin and George Strickler, who served as directors of LCDC's New Orleans office after Richard Sobol left. See also Hilbink, "Filling the Void."

10. Hilbink, "Filling the Void."

2. ARMED ESCORTS

1. Kim Lacy Rogers provides a well-researched account of the history of the civil rights movement in New Orleans and CORE's relationship with Collins, Douglas, and Elie in *Righteous Lives* (New York: New York University Press, 1993).

2. Rogers, *Righteous Lives*, 55.

3. Rogers, *Righteous Lives*, 67.

4. Thomas Hilbink wrote a moving tribute on the death of Henry Schwarzschild in "A Moralist in a Legalist World: A Memorial Essay for Henry Schwarzschild," *Review of Law and Social Change* 23 (1997): 199.

5. Phone interview with Richard Sobol on March 5, 1997.

6. Interview with Lolis Elie, April 29, 1997.

3. KLAN VIOLENCE AND THE DEACONS

1. See Roy Reed, "The Deacons, Too, Ride by Night," *New York Times Magazine*, August 15, 1965, 10. Also, Adam Fairclough writes that an FBI report written at the time disputes this number, asserting that there were no more than three Deacons chapters (*Race and Democracy: The Civil Rights Struggle in Louisiana, 1915–1971* [Athens: University of Georgia Press, 1995], 357) . Fairclough's book is a useful source for anyone studying the early days of the Bogalusa civil rights movement.

2. See Reed, "The Deacons," and Fairclough, *Race and Democracy*, 357.

3. Fairclough, *Race and Democracy*, 357.

4. Fairclough, *Race and Democracy*, 357, supports this as well.

5. In *Race and Democracy*, chapter 12, Fairclough describes the violence and conflict of 1964 and 1965.

6. *United States v Original Knights of the Ku Klux Klan*, 250 F. Supp. 330 (ED La. 1965).

7. Jack Bass, *Unlikely Heroes* (New York: Simon and Schuster, 1981), offers a tribute to Judge Wisdom and to several other remarkable Southern judges whose decisions upholding the rights of African Americans incurred the wrath of local politicians. Judge Wisdom died in May 1999, just shy of his ninety-fourth birthday.

8. *United States v Original Knights of the Ku Klux Klan*, 250 F. Supp. 330, 334.

9. *United States v Original Knights of the Ku Klux Klan*, 250 F. Supp. 330, 341.

10. *United States v Original Knights of the Ku Klux Klan*, 250 F. Supp. 330, 343.

11. *New York Times*, September 7, 1965, 26.

12. *United States v Original Knights of the Ku Klux Klan*, 250 F. Supp. 330, n. 1.

13. *Hicks v Knight*, Civil Action No. 15727, filed in the United States District Court, Eastern District of Louisiana, New Orleans Division, 1965. Judge Christenberry was also a member of the three-judge panel that decided the *Original Knights of the Ku Klux Klan* case.

14. *New York Times*, July 17, 1965, 39.

15. *New York Times*, December 29, 1965, 18.

16. *New York Times*, December 29, 1965, 18.

17. *New York Times*, December 30, 1965, 6, 11.

18. Fairclough, *Race and Democracy*, 359.

19. Reed, "The Deacons," 11, and Fairclough, *Race and Democracy*, 357–59.

20. Fairclough, *Race and Democracy*, 359.

21. Reed, "The Deacons," 11.

4. FIRST COUSINS

1. Interview with Gayle Jenkins, May 5, 1997.

2. Adam Fairclough describes the events leading up to CORE's appearance in Bogalusa in *Race and Democracy: The Civil Rights Struggle in Louisiana, 1915–1971* (Athens: University of Georgia Press, 1995), 350–55.

3. Interview with Lolis Elie, April 29, 1997.

4. Interview with Robert Hicks, April 21, 1996.

5. Interview on April 29, 1997.

6. STEPPING OFF THE SIDELINES

1. Howell Raines, *My Soul Is Rested* (New York: Putnam, 1977), 420.

7. WELCOME TO NEW ORLEANS

1. Kim Lacy Rogers, *Righteous Lives* (New York: New York University Press, 1993), 20.
2. *Dombrowski v Pfister*, 380 US 479, 495 (1965).
3. *Dombrowski v Pfister*, 380 US 479.

8. LITIGATING THE END TO SEGREGATION

1. *New York Times*, September 2, 1965, 15.
2. See *United States v Jefferson County Board of Education*, 372 F2d 836, 888 (5th Cir 1966). For the story of an African American family in Sunflower County, Mississippi, who courageously sent their children to an all-white school in 1965, see Constance Curry, *Silver Rights* (New York: Harcourt Brace, 1996).
3. *New York Times*, September 13, 1966, 29.
4. *New York Times*, September 15, 1966, 28.
5. *United States v Jefferson County Board of Education*, 372 F2d 836.
6. *United States v Jefferson County Board of Education*, 372 F2d 836, 849.
7. *United States v Jefferson County Board of Education*, 372 F2d 836, 847. In later years, Judge Wisdom regarded this case as one that helped set in place the concept of affirmative action.
8. 28 USC § 1443.
9. 384 US 808 (1966).
10. *Whatley v City of Vidalia*, 399 F2d 521 (5th Cir 1968).

9. HIROSHIMA VIGIL

1. *Aronson v Giarrusso*, 436 F2d 955, 957 (1971).
2. *Aronson v Giarrusso*, 436 F2d 955, 957.
3. *New York Times*, June 5, 1965, 15.

4. *New York Times*, July 11, 1965, 46.

5. *New York Times*, July 9, 1965, 1, and July 10, 1965, 23.

11. AN UNWARRANTED TOUCHING

1. Robert Sherrill, *Gothic Politics in the Deep South: Stars of the New Confederacy* (New York: Grossman, 1968), 7.

2. *Political Profiles: The Kennedy Years* (New York: Facts on File, 1976), 408.

3. *Political Profiles: The Johnson Years* (New York: Facts on File, 1976), 475.

4. *Political Profiles: The Kennedy Years* (New York: Facts on File, 1976), 408.

14. *SOBOL V PEREZ*

1. *Sobol v Perez*, 289 F.Supp. 392, 402 (ED La. 1968).

2. Deposition of Leander Perez Sr. on August 11, 1967, taken at 430 Maritime Building, New Orleans, Louisiana, 63–64.

3. Perez deposition. All subsequent quotations are taken from this source.

17. "WE'LL BRING YOUR FREEDOM BACK TO YOU"

1. Statement of A.Z. Young, president of the Bogalusa Voters League, July 21, 1967.

2. Statement of A.Z. Young, July 21, 1967.

3. Statement of A.Z. Young, July 21, 1967.

4. *New York Times*, July 25, 1967, 17.

5. Actually, beginning with the early 1960s sit-ins and demonstrations in Baton Rouge, Southern University had a history of expelling and otherwise disciplining students who participated in protests against segregation. August Meier and Elliott Rudwick, *CORE: A Study in the Civil Rights Movement, 1942–1968* (New York: Oxford University Press, 1973), 108,167.

6. *New York Times*, August 20, 1967, 40.

7. *New York Times*, August 19, 1967, 12.

8. *Washington Post*, August 19, 1967, A2.

9. *New York Times*, August 19, 1967, 1.

10. *New York Times*, August 19, 1967, 1.

11. *New York Times*, August 20, 1967, 40.
12. *Washington Post*, August 21, 1967, A4.

18. MOVING ON

1. *Duncan v Louisiana*, 391 US 145 (1968).
2. *Duncan v Perez*, 321 F.Supp. 181, 184 (ED La. 1970).
3. *Duncan v Perez*, 445 F2d 557 (5th Cir 1971).

AFTERWORD

1. A longer account of this incident and my response to it appears in *Phi Delta Kappan*, November 1995, 252.

INDEX

Acme Cafe (Bogalusa, Louisiana), test integration of, 42–44
AFL-CIO, as plaintiff in Crown Zellerbach segregation suit, 76
African Americans: attempts to integrate schools, 37, 71–75, 129, 153; Black Power movement and, 6–7, 127–28, 137–38, 144–46; comparison of Southern-bred blacks and Northern white activists, 7–8; participation in Mardi Gras krewe parades, 120, 121–24; violence against by police and white civilians, 27–33, 60, 135–36; white Bogalusa schools' refusal to hire as teachers, 74
American Civil Liberties Union (ACLU), 15
American Jewish Committee, 15
American Jewish Congress, 15
Amsterdam, Anthony (Tony), 78, 115
Anti-Communist Christian Association, as front for Bogalusa Klan, 28–29
Aronson, Henry, 12–13, 165n5
Austin, Henry, 84–87

Bailey, D'Army, 10–11, 13, 58–59
Barbie dolls, lack of minority culture versions, 159–60
Baton Rouge, 1967 march to, 138–47

beach, public, attempt to integrate on Lake Pontchartrain, 50, 51–56, 150
Bell, Murphy, 63
Berkeley High School (Berkeley, California), 159
Black Panthers, 26
Black Power, rise of, 6–7, 127–28, 137–38, 144–46
blacks. *See* African Americans
Blackwell, Unita, 12
"Bloody Sunday," assaults on Selma to Montgomery marchers, 6
"Bloody Wednesday," police violence in Bogalusa, 31–32
Bogalusa, Louisiana: background of, 21–22; history of town violence, 26–33; integrating its schools, 71–75; picketing of white-owned businesses, 35, 38, 104, 105, 128. *See also* Crown Zellerbach paper mill; Hicks, Robert; Jenkins, Gayle; Young, A. Z.
Bogalusa Voters League (BVL): as African American civil rights organization, 27, 40, 45; coordination of 1967 summer marches, 134–35, 138
Bourbon Street (New Orleans), 64–65
boycotts, of white-owned stores in Bogalusa, 35, 38, 104, 105, 128
Bresnick, David, 80, 82, 89
Bronstein, Alvin, 113–18

171

Equal Employment Opportunity Commission (EEOC), job test guidelines, 77

Farmer, James, 7, 138
FBI (Federal Bureau of Investigation): perceived role in 1960s enforcement of civil rights, 12–13, 41; report on reputed weapons carried by Bogalusa Deacons, 33
Fifth Circuit Court of Appeals, 21, 74, 79, 82, 154
Flambeaux, black torch paraders during Mardi Gras, 121–22
Fleischer, Hugh, 141
Franklinton, Louisiana (Washington Parish seat), march to by Bogalusa African Americans, 83–84, 134–38
freedom of choice plan, for school integration, 71–75
Freedom Riders, 5
"freedom schools," in 1964 Mississippi, 5–6
Freedom Summer, 1964, 5–6, 15
French Quarter (New Orleans), 2, 64–66, 69, 83; Mardi Gras and, 119, 120, 124
funeral, jazz, New Orleans, 91

Garden District (New Orleans), 70–71
Gideon's Trumpet (Lewis), 101
Gideon v Wainwright, 101
Gold, Sam (fictional name), 130–33
Goodman, Andrew, 6, 31
Gutman, Jeremiah, 18–19, 20, 34

Haley, Richard, 73, 95
Halpin, Stanley, 156, 166n9
Health, Education and Welfare, U.S. Department of, perceived role in 1960s enforcement of civil rights, 12, 71–72
Heebe, Frederick J. R. (federal judge), 73–74, 76–77, 136, 156

Hicks, Charles, 138–39, 146, 169n5
Hicks, Gregory, 30
Hicks, Robert, 86n; and Bogalusa to Baton Rouge march, 140; and Bogalusa to Franklinton march, 134–35, 138; as leader in Bogalusa civil rights movement, 27, 30, 34, 39–42, 45; as lead plaintiff in suit against Crown Zellerbach, 76, 77
Hicks, Valeria (Jack), 32, 39
Hicks v Knight, 30, 39, 167n13
Hilbink, Thomas, 166n4
Hill, Hattie Mae, 85–86
Hiroshima vigil, photographing of participants by police, 80–82
Honigsberg, Peter Jan: background in New York City, 3–5, 7; bailing out picketers in Bogalusa, 106–9; in Berkeley, 157–61; Dow Chemical demonstration and subsequent NYU Law School's attempted sanctions, 149–52; drive through South to Chicago, 84, 87–88; influence of parents' background as refugee Austrian Jews, 3–4, 161–62; integrating beach at Lake Pontchartrain, 50, 51–57; marches of 1967, 134–48; participation in test integration of Acme Cafe, 42–44
Hoover, J. Edgar, 12
Houston, Charles, 14–15, 165n6

Inc. Fund (NAACP Legal Defense and Educational Fund), 9–10, 12, 14
Indians (Native Americans), African Americans masquerading as during Mardi Gras revels, 122–24
International Brotherhood of Pulp, Sulphite and Paper Mills Workers, 76

Jackson, Mississippi, 38
jazz funeral, New Orleans, 91
Jelinck, Don, 112

Text: 10/15 Janson
Display: Janson
Composition: Binghamton Valley Composition
Printing and binding: Haddon Craftsmen
Index: Indi-Indexes